Making a Difference

USING LITERATURE TO CHANGE CHILDREN'S LIVES

Kendall Hunt
publishing company

LAURA BATES

Cover image © Shutterstock, Inc.

Kendall Hunt
publishing company

www.kendallhunt.com
Send all inquiries to:
4050 Westmark Drive
Dubuque, IA 52004-1840

Copyright © 2016 by Kendall Hunt Publishing Company

ISBN 978-1-4652-9987-1

Printed in the United States of America

Contents

Foreword

I first met Laura Bates in 2003, and at that time, she had just begun working on her book *Shakespeare Saved My Life: Ten Years in Solitary with the Bard*. We had both fallen in love with Shakespeare and discovered how powerfully his words could resonate for people who lived in the darkest places. I produced and directed plays with women in a Massachusetts state prison where they could express their deepest selves and feel heard in front of an audience, trying on the language of Portia or demanding to be accepted as Shylock. Laura had the gumption to work with men in solitary confinement where they could only speak lines to each other through small slots in their doors. These men were considered unredeemable by many, but Laura begged to differ. She found that art had the power to help people transcend their bars and think differently about themselves, their actions, and how they wanted to live the rest of their days, even if it was to be in a supermax prison. She found that words had the power to help men change their lives by changing their attitudes and their thinking.

Language indeed can be a gateway to change. I have seen this firsthand through the program I have worked in for nearly twenty-five years, Changing Lives Through Literature (CLTL).

CLTL is an alternative sentencing program offered through the courts that puts probationers in a democratic conversation with judges and probation officers. Founded in Massachusetts in 1991 by a judge and a college professor, we have been able to run programs in Connecticut, Indiana, Virginia, Kansas, Texas, California, New York, Illinois, Rhode Island, Maine, and Arizona, as well as in Massachusetts. Practitioners from England have also adapted the program to use in prisons.

The concept is simple but profound: probationers can gain valuable perspectives and reasoned understandings by reading and discussing good books. Each class (seven to eight over a semester) is not only attended by a facilitator/professor, a judge, a probation officer, and a group of probationer students, but in the discussions there are no right or wrong answers, and all ideas and comments are treated equally. We work as a team to help probationers return to a more deeply examined life. We have graduations in courtrooms: success where they once felt shame. With a substantial return to education, a deeper understanding of self and life's possibilities, better behavioral choices, improved relationships with family and jobs, and according to the *Journal of Offender Rehabilitation*, CLTL shows a substantial improvement in not returning to crime.

With *Making a Difference: Using Literature to Change Children's Lives*, Bates, who is also a professor of Children's Literature as well as a Shakespeare scholar, is again tackling what she is so capable and prepared to do—take on helping more of our citizens with an idea similar to CLTL's. Many of our young people, for a variety of reasons—be it economics or race, have been prevented from easy access to the written word. Many face unfamiliarity with deciphering text. Some have not yet found their way into a book, a stage performance, a photograph, or in some cases, a paragraph. As teachers, we cannot change the economics, and most often cannot dispel the discrimination that many children face; but we can equip them more fully to take part in an ever-changing world. We can do our part to give them a leg up.

With *Making a Difference*, Bates has committed herself to help future teachers better serve our youth. In these pages, she offers explicit attempts for practitioners to delve into social issues and engage young people in understanding their own humanity through a deeper experience of language. Those we call "at risk," may often be blocked from their deeper selves, but as I have seen through Changing Lives, what a reader can so often discover in books is a new appreciation of one's own talents as well as a more insightful connection to others. Such readers can change thinking, choices, behavior, and thus, their lives.

This book is a needed addition to a school's curriculum which so often leaves out the social justice aspect of children's experience. Lessons often approach techniques to help teachers create change but do not have the important goal of developing compassion. In these pages, Laura Bates offers a key for teachers to unlock hearts as well as minds.

Jean Trounstine, *author/editor of six books,*
is the co-founder of the women's branch of
Changing Lives Through Literature

Introduction: Making a Difference

"At what age did your criminal career begin?" I asked.

Their responses took me by surprise.

Dustin: "Twelve. Started off with runaways, criminal mischief."

Steve: "Ten. Playing hooky from school, selling dope."

Larry: "Ten. Stealing from K-Mart."

Jon: "Eight. Keying cars, vandalism."

James "Eight. Stealing pop from the store whenever I was thirsty from playing ball."

Patrick: "Seven—."

Me: "Seven?"

Patrick: "Seven. Calling in false fires, out past curfew, drinking under age."

Me: *"Seven?!"*

Kevin, the only prisoner in the group who was not serving a murder sentence, summed it up by saying, "What a child experiences between the ages of seven and ten will determine his actions as a teenager and an adult." (Bates 203–204)

This excerpt from my book *Shakespeare Saved My Life: Ten Years in Solitary with the Bard* (Sourcebooks, 2013) presents a conversation I had with a group of adult prisoners who had committed murder as juveniles. Patrick went from criminal mischief at age seven to murder at eighteen . . . and a life sentence. Jon went from vandalism at eight to a double homicide at eighteen . . . and two fifty-five-year sentences. Larry went from shoplifting at ten to murder at seventeen . . . and life without parole. Steve went from selling dope at ten to killing two of his teenaged partners at age sixteen, receiving two eighty-year sentences. James went from shoplifting at eight to murder during a robbery with a buddy at age sixteen, receiving a life sentence. Dustin, in just two years, went from criminal mischief at twelve to murder at fourteen. Yes, *fourteen!* And he received a sentence of 199 years.

This conversation was an eye-opening experience for me. And it has informed the way I teach children's literature ever since. For more than twenty years, I had taught Shakespeare in prison. For more than twenty years, I had taught Children's Literature on campus. It wasn't until that conversation that I saw a connection. Previously I had assumed that the teenaged years were the time for intervention for "at risk" juveniles. But in conversations with these prisoners I learned that the formative years are much earlier. The time for intervention isn't high school. It's elementary school.

You may be working with seven-year-olds who are calling in false fires, staying out past curfew, or drinking under age. Eight-year-olds who are stealing pop or keying cars. Ten-year-olds playing hooky from school or, perhaps, even selling dope. And twelve-year-olds running away from home. Will they leave your classroom and go on to become murderers before they graduate from high school? That may be up to you.

You shouldn't assume that it's only the children in inner-city schools that engage in juvenile criminal behaviors. Suburban and rural schools have their share of "at-risk" students as well. It's not always the obviously troubled kids who are engaging in such behaviors. How will you be able to identify the Patrick or the Larry or the Dustin in your class? And how should you intervene?

I asked those adult prisoners to recall their formative years in elementary school and to make suggestions for my students who were preparing to become elementary school teachers. One suggestion was: "Make each child feel special."

But if every child is special, then no child is special. So, how can you do that? Help each child find his or her own unique way to be special, to shine in their own personal strength, or to overcome a weakness, such as shyness.

Even well-intentioned interventions can backfire. Jon grew up in a middle-class suburban household with two loving parents. Yet, as he told us in the quotation at the top of this chapter, his criminal career began as early as eight, with vandalism and keying cars. At the age of eighteen, just a few weeks before his high school graduation, he went to the mall to hang out with his girlfriend and ended up killing two people. What happened that led him from juvenile mischief to cold-blooded murder?

In the fifth grade, he had a teacher who had heard of his reputation as a trouble-maker. To keep him from being a disturbance to the rest of the class, she had him spend the entire semester in the back of a room, behind a partition. That experience resulted in his rejection of the teacher, of his schoolwork, of school in general. Eventually, that led to drugs and violence. In Jon's words, "Stick me behind a partition, and I grow up and kill someone."

FEATURE

10 Million Children

In addition to children who are committing crimes, consider the situation of children whose parents are criminals.

When James, quoted earlier, came to prison at the age of sixteen, he had just learned that his girlfriend was pregnant. He ended up being paroled at the age of forty-eight, having served thirty-two years of his sentence. When he returned home, where would you guess his thirty-two-year-old daughter was? That's right: in prison.

Ten million children in America have a parent or other family member with a prison record. Indiana ranks second in the nation, with one child in eight. In certain counties, that number is much higher. What kind of role models are these children growing up with?

According to a youth.gov Web site, 2.7 million (or one in twenty-eight) children currently have an incarcerated parent. More than 10 million children have experienced parental incarceration at some point in their childhoods. Given these numbers, there may be a child in your classroom or school who has an incarcerated parent. Women are a fast growing part of the correctional population (the number of incarcerated women increased at nearly 1.5 times the rate of men between 1980 and 2010). If your student's mother has been incarcerated, there is an increased likelihood of instability in that student's home and an increased chance that student may enter foster care or have to move to another caregiver's home (such as a grandparent).

The Web site includes helpful materials for teachers, such as:

Five Things to Know About Children Who Have an Incarcerated Parent
1. Children with an incarcerated parent may be in your classroom.   2. Having an incarcerated parent is recognized as an "adverse childhood experience."   3. Children with a parent in prison may be subject to stereotypes and subconscious negative assumptions.   4. Be sensitive to certain trigger issues.   5. Be aware of what researchers call the "conspiracy of silence."
Source: http://youth.gov/youth-topics/children-of-incarcerated-parents/federal-tools-resources/tip-sheet-teachers

Finding Their Bliss

What did you want to be when you grew up?

Mythologist and author, Joseph Campbell, believed that what we enjoyed as children will determine what makes us happy as adults. Campbell said, "If you follow your bliss, you put yourself on a kind of track that has been there all the while, waiting for you, and the life that you ought to be living is the one you are living. Wherever you are—if you are following your bliss, you are enjoying that refreshment, that life within you, all the time."

The group of prisoners quoted earlier addressed this question, and again their answers are surprising and eye-opening for educators or anyone working with children.

Ironically, one of them had wanted to be a police officer. Others had aspirations to become fire-fighters or veterinarians or even astronauts. Whether realistic or idealistic, they all had goals. All except Larry. He said that he could not remember ever, at any age as he was growing up, to have had any aspirations whatsoever, except impressing his buddies through his criminal behavior.

Another example from the prisoners I've worked with represented the opposite extreme. Phil had a goal, but it was not a positive one. Growing up in a hardcore inner-city neighborhood without a father, he looked up to the men in his 'hood who seemed to be the most successful. They had nice cars, lots of money and women. But they were professional hit men. Phil said that from the age of five, that was his goal: to grow up and become a hit man. And he did. "I grew up," said Phil, "and I killed three people. I got $100,000 . . . and three life sentences."

The lesson for educators is to recall Campbell's theory, along with Larry's example, and ensure that their young students have desires and aspirations. The lesson from prisoners like Phil is to make sure that the goals they pursue are positive ones.

On another day and in another type of lock-down facility, I asked a group of teenaged girls the "what did you want to be" question. There were some princesses, ballerinas, and a Hannah Montana or two. The last girl to speak quietly said, "Assassin." And she had already committed murder at the age of twelve. Yes, *twelve.*

FEATURE

Gateway Crimes

Most adult killers don't begin with childhood aspirations to become assassins or hit men. But some childish behaviors, such as vandalism and shoplifting, have been shown to be "gateway" crimes. Animal abuse is a common precursor to violence on human victims.

In a Web site titled, "Animal Cruelty and Human Violence: A Documented Connection," the Humane Society of the United States addresses the question: Is there a connection between animal abuse and criminal violence?

A number of studies have drawn links between the abuse of animals and violence against people. A 2001–2004 study by the Chicago Police Department "revealed a startling propensity for offenders charged with crimes against animals to commit other violent offenses toward human victims." Of those arrested for animal crimes, 65% had been arrested for battery against another person. Of thirty-six convicted multiple murderers questioned in one study, 46% admitted committing acts of animal torture as adolescents. And of seven school shootings that took place across the country between 1997 and 2001, all involved boys who had previously committed acts of animal cruelty.

http://www.humanesociety.org/issues/abuse_neglect/qa/cruelty_violence_connection_faq.html

Using Literature to Change Childrens' Lives

So, given the problem, what can a teacher do? What can literature do?

As a professor of literature, my primary expertise lies in the literature itself, and this book will provide a solid foundation in each of the main genres of children's literature. While I may not be a sociologist or psychologist, I do recognize that any work of literature presented to a child provides the opportunity to teach him or her more than basic reading skills. Your choice of literature, and the way in which you present it, carries a powerful potential for changing the life of that child.

Jean Trounstine and others have demonstrated the uses of literature in rehabilitation of convicted adults and juveniles. See *Finding a Voice: The Practice of Changing Lives through Literature,* co-written by Trounstine and English professor Robert Waxler (2005). The program involves "choosing literature with themes that resonate for a group, literature that speaks to readers' underlying issues. It is finding ways to engage the disengaged, giving voice to those that feel unheard . . ." (Trounstine 6).

For work with children in particular, see *Bibliotherapy* (2015) by Dr. Linda Karges-Bone and *Bibliotherapy: When Kids Need Books,* by Amy Recob (2008). My own work with Shakespeare in prison has shown that literature can create a safe place in which any reader, adult or child, can examine the actions, behaviors, and motivations of the literary characters and then use that analysis to examine their own character.

This book presents four units, for children from kindergarten to middle school, dealing with four main genres of children's literature. Each unit does double duty: teaching the literature while providing an opportunity to explore important issues in the child's social development.

Unit One: Picture Books

As noted above, research indicates that it is common among convicted killers to find that they abused animals at a young age. This unit is designed to inspire affinity and respect for animals, nature, and all living things, with the expectation that this will lead to respect for human life as well.

Unit Two: Fairy Tales

Diversity is an important consideration in education today, as classrooms embrace students from diverse ethnic and cultural backgrounds. Looking at universal elements of international fairy tales shows children that we are more alike than different, no matter where we live or where our ancestors came from.

Unit Three: Children's Theatre

At-risk children are often kinesthetic learners, responding well to classroom activities in which they can express themselves physically. Theatre is a wonderful vehicle through which they can act out, and putting themselves into another's role gives them the opportunity to empathize with another's perspective. Additionally, this project involves teamwork, cooperation, overcoming shyness, and encourages creativity.

Unit Four: Adolescent Fiction

This unit expressly addresses the issue of juvenile delinquency, but it does so through the medium of literature by examining literary characters such as Tom Sawyer or Huck Finn in nineteenth century fiction, or more contemporary examples such as Byron Watson (*The Watsons Go to Birmingham 1963*) or Claudia Kincaid (*From the Mixed-Up Files of Mrs. Basil E. Frankweiler)*.

This book is designed for Elementary Education students, pre-service teachers, and anyone working with or interested in children. In this book, you will learn ways in which you can change children's lives through literature.

Unit One

Picture Books

(Grades K–2)

Introduction

> Even when they are not intended to do so, picture books provide children with some of their earliest takes on morality, taste, and basic cultural knowledge, including messages about gender, race, and class. They apply a stock of images for children's mental museums. Read by loving parents and respected adults or other siblings, they stand firm against later experience.
>
> —Ellen Handler Spitz, *Inside Picture Books*

Words are powerful. In picture books—as in poetry—this effect is enhanced. In literary forms in which there are relatively few words, each word carries that much more weight.

What was your favorite picture book as a child? Which one do you remember most and why?

I surveyed several experts on the subject, those who have taught me the most about this field: my nine grandchildren, now ranging in ages from ten to twenty-five. Here are some of the picture books that had the most impact on them:

Goodnight Moon

The Lorax

The Little Engine that Could

Oh, the Places You'll Go

What do these books have in common?

Notice that many of them featured animals, fantasy creatures, toys, or other forms of "sympathetic" characters. We'll discuss characters in more detail later in this unit (see Lesson Three).

Now consider the book you chose. What was it about the book? Did it have a sympathetic character? Or, was it something about the way the book was presented to you? The way it was read to you by a teacher or parent?

Text + Readers = Meaning.

This equation from the branch of literary analysis known as Reader Response Theory suggests that each individual reader brings to any text, his or her own background through which "meaning" is constructed. You and I could read the same book and come away with two different meanings, each one equally valid.

With picture books, this equation is complicated, as meaning is often mediated by a third element. Whenever a picture book is read aloud to a child, the meaning constructed by that child is very much influenced by the manner in which the book is presented. The myriad ways in which you can shape meaning when you read aloud will be discussed in detail later in this unit (see Lesson Three).

Another useful equation to bear in mind is:

Text + Art = Picture Book.

Picture books are more than illustrated stories, or stories with illustrations. In picture books, the text and the graphics carry *equal* weight. A good exercise to test this theory is to read a book to a child without ever letting him or her look at the pictures. You'll see how much is lost.

Conversely, show a group of children the pages of a picture with the text obscured, and have them make up their own captions. You'll see what a wide range of interpretations they'll have for the illustrations.

When appropriately combined, the art and text each enhance the meaning of one another, in terms of tone and context clues for challenging words (we'll discuss context clues in more detail later in this unit; see Lesson Three).

Picture books play a key role in language acquisition in an emergent-literate population: they teach children how to read. Beyond that, when they are coupled with an effective presenter, they can also teach children to *love* to read.

Furthermore, the choice of books that you present can teach an additional lesson.

Statistics have shown that it is common among adult killers to discover that as children they had a history of abusing animals, some of them being as heartless as to kill their own pet.

Ultimately, in this unit, you will teach a secondary lesson: to love and respect all living creatures.

THE PROJECT

Create an original picture book in collaboration with a child.

Lesson One: Choose a Child

Lesson Two: Consult the Caldecotts

Lesson Three: Read to Your Child

Lesson Four: Craft the Storyline

Lesson Five: Get Anthropomorphic

Lesson Six: Write the Text

Lesson Seven: Create the Illustrations

Lesson Eight: Design the Pages

Lesson Nine: Research and Reflect

Lesson Ten: Prepare to Teach

Lesson

©cs333/Shutterstock.com

Choose a Child

The first step:

Think of one child you know that you might be able to work with during the next three weeks, ideally more than once. In selecting the appropriate child for this project, consider the following:

- ► a relative may be harder to work with

- ► your own child may be the hardest

- ► an unfamiliar child may pose a different kind of challenge

- ► working with more than one child can be distracting

The next step:

Once you have identified an appropriate child, discuss the project with him/her—and his/her parent[s]—as soon as possible. You might even take a moment right now to send a text or email. You want to:

- ► Briefly describe your project

   But don't go into too much detail at this stage. You want the child to be an equal partner in the creative act.

Don't say:

"I have to create a picture book for my class, and I thought we should use a puppy as the main character because I know you like puppies."

Why not?

That's right—you are providing too much direction. Even though it might seem like a good idea to acknowledge your child's favorite animal, you should let the choice of animal be his/ her own idea. You might be surprised! The child who loves puppies may choose to use a cat— or a dinosaur.

▶ Arrange a time to get together

This may be the most challenging part of this project. If your child lives far away and you are unable to visit in person, consider collaborating with him/her via technology, such as:

— Skype or Facetime. These multimedia technologies allow you to both see and hear one another as you discuss story ideas or select appropriate graphics.

— Telephone. You can talk out initial ideas for characters and storyline by phone.

— Email. Using attachments, you could send graphics or page designs back and forth.

Whether you work together face-to-face or via technology, it is important to have enough time, free of distractions or interruptions. Ideally, you should get together more than once as your project is developed over several shorter work sessions.

The final step:

Describe the child using the following worksheet. You may not know everything about him/her at this stage, but you should fill out each category of the worksheet with your best guess. If you don't know what pets he/she has had, you might find it a good learning experience if you make an assumption that he/she has had dogs, cats, and goldfish, and then discover that he/she has never had any pets at all. Or perhaps you underestimate (or overestimate) his/her reading or writing ability.

Once you get to know more about your child, by speaking with him/her as well with parents or teachers, you can make any corrections to your worksheet to more accurately describe your child and prepare the best possible book for, and with, him/her.

Lesson

©cs333/Shutterstock.com

Consult the Caldecotts

The first step:

Before you can create your own original "award-winning" picture book, you need to look at some of the best books ever published in this genre. The gold standard is the annual Caldecott Medal, established in 1937. You can access information about the award and a comprehensive list of annual winners through the Association for Library Service to Children Web site at http://www.ala.org/alsc/awardsgrants/ bookmedia/caldecottmedal/caldecottmedal"dsgrants/bookmedia/caldecottmedal/caldecottmedal.

Some notable books from recent years include:

2015:   *The Adventures of Beekle: The Unimaginary Friend* by Dan Santat (Little, Brown and Company, a division of Hachette Book Group, Inc.)

2012:   *A Ball for Daisy* by Chris Raschka (Schwartz & Wade Books, an imprint of Random House Children's Books, a division of Random House, Inc.)

2010:   *The Lion & the Mouse* by Jerry Pinkney (Little, Brown and Company)

2005:   *Kitten's First Full Moon* by Kevin Henkes (Greenwillow Books/HarperCollins Publishers)

2003:   *My Friend Rabbit* by Eric Rohmann (Roaring Brook Press/Millbrook Press)

Some "classics" from earlier years include:

1942:   *Make Way for Ducklings* by Robert McCloskey (Viking)

1956:   *Frog Went A-Courtin'*, illustrated by Feodor Rojankovsky; text: retold by John Langstaff (Harcourt)

1964:   *Where the Wild Things Are* by Maurice Sendak (Harper)

1970:   *Sylvester and the Magic Pebble* by William Steig (Windmill Books)

1988:   *Owl Moon*, illustrated by John Schoenherr; text: Jane Yolen (Philomel)

Examining books such as these will give you a good idea of what qualities make a successful picture book. Additionally, because they also focus on animals or nature, they could serve as models for your storyline as well as your graphic design.

The next step:

Research some of the books online, through sites such as Amazon,com, where you can begin to analyze the cover design and title. Some authors, such as Kevin Henkes, have their own Web site: kevinhenkes. com. Here you can find more information about the books and even useful teaching tools for educators. Ask yourself questions such as:

THE TITLE

Is it compelling and evocative, or confusing and unclear?

Based on the title alone, what do you expect the book to be about?

THE COVER

Are the graphics impressionistic cartoons, realistic drawings, or photographs?

How are the animals portrayed?

Is the tone happy and inviting, or ferocious and off-putting?

What is the background?

Is it colorful, or black and white?

The final step:

Locate one or more of the books in the library so that you can read them in full and examine the interior page design and overall storyline. If you are unable to locate Caldecott books, browse the library's picture book holdings for other books that deal with animals and nature.

Lesson

©cs333/Shutterstock.com

Read to Your Child

The first step:

Naturally, you'll want to read a few books, Caldecotts or others, to serve as models and inspiration for your own book. Since your child is your co-author, he or she will benefit as much as you will from reading model books.

Arrange a quiet time to read together. Assuming that your child is approximately the age of your intended audience, from pre-school to grade 2 or so, you'll probably be the one doing most of the reading. Remember our equation:

$$\text{Text} + \text{Readers} = \text{Meaning.}$$

Be aware that as the reader, you will constantly be "mediating" your child's understanding of, and response to, the books.

The next step:

How can you influence your child's construction of meaning? Let us count the ways!

I often ask my students to come up with a list of 100. That's not a typo for "10." There truly are 100 ways in which you influence your children when you read—at least!

Here's a true story. Many years ago, Children's Literature at my university was a class that students from any major could take for general education credit. As such, it attracted a large number of students who had little to no sincere interest in the topic, but assumed it would be an easy class. One such student, who shall remain nameless (because I don't recall his name), began his class presentation on the picture book unit with these honest words:

"So I went to the library and got a stupid picture book and then I read to my kid and he thought the book was _____."

<small>Fill in the blank.</small>

If you said "stupid," you're right. What other conclusion could the child draw when the adult reading to him—the authority figure—prefaced his reading by announcing that the book was "stupid"? And, yes, that was the word he used. Although I don't remember the student's name, I do remember the word, and the lesson we all learned from his example. The room was ablaze with the lightbulbs going off over forty-five students' heads.

Of course, you would never be guilty of such a glaring faux pas yourself. But what are some of the more subtle ways in which you influence the child's interpretation of the book you are reading? See if you can come up with a list of 100. Or, at least, 10.

Now consult the list I've provided. You may feel that the first few are obvious, but what about some of the others?

1. Ask the child to predict what the book will be about based on the title or cover
2. Ask questions at key moments in the reading
3. Look at the seating arrangement for you and your child
4. Be aware of your body language
5. Read outdoors (especially a book about nature)
6. Vary your enthusiasm
7. Vary your pace
8. Vary your intensity
9. Emphasize key words
10. Don't be afraid of Silence (i.e., a pause, to elicit anticipation for the next word)

The list goes on and on, but you get the idea.

The final step:

An excellent strategy for emergent readers is prediction. You can employ this strategy beginning with the cover, pausing at key moments in the book, and especially after the entire book has been read. Consider asking your child to predict what will happen next to one or more of the characters, perhaps even brainstorming a sequel or adaptation to the book. To encourage his imagination, you could ask for alternative endings. Come up with as many as possible, and then analyze them. Is the author's ending the best one? Why or why not?

Lesson

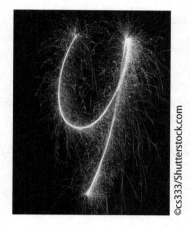

©cs333/Shutterstock.com

Craft the Storyline

The first step:

Let's begin by focusing on your characters. You already know who your main character is: your child. The description worksheet that you filled out in Lesson One will be helpful in creating a character based on your actual child. Consider putting his name in the title: *The Adventures of Billy and His Faithful Pal Bozo.*

But who is Bozo, his faithful pal? Here, too, your Lesson One worksheet will come in handy. You could use a pet he has had, or currently has. Some children, especially at this early age, may not have ever had any kind of pet. In that case, you should encourage your child to tell you what kind of pet he has always wanted. The creative experience of going on an "adventure" with this desired pet can have a beneficial, cathartic effect. Another possibility, if your child is especially imaginative, could be to create a kind of pet that he could never have in real life:

> an alligator, as in Mo Willem's *Hooray for Abigail and Her Alligator*
>
> a dinosaur, as in Marcus Sedaka's *My Pet Dinosaur*
>
> or a made-up creature, as in Maurice Sendak's *Where the Wild Things Are*
>
> even a plant or tree, as in Shel Silverstein's *The Giving Tree.*

It doesn't matter if his companion is real or fictional; what matters is that it invokes empathy. It is a character he cares about, or better yet, comes to care about by the end of the story. For this, you might consider the special challenge of writing about "icky" worms, "scary" snakes, or whatever animal your child has a phobia about or aversion to.

Shakespeare's *King Lear* contains this classic line:

> "As flies to wanton boys are we to the gods.
>
> They kill us for their sport."

Through this unit, you want to teach your students—even your "wanton boys" (or girls)—to respect all living creatures, even flies.

Your goal is to not only tell a good story, but also to create empathy.

The next step:

How can you create empathy? Rather than beginning with two characters who are already best buddies, you might consider a friendship that develops between two unlikely parties as the story develops. Perhaps they even start out with an antagonistic relationship (think of Harry Potter and Hermione, Belle and her Beast, or even Curious George, the mischievous monkey who first meets his new friend by stealing the man's big yellow hat).

Dan Santat's 2014 picture book, *The Adventures of Beekle*, relates the sad story of Beekle, an imaginary friend in search of a real child who needs him (rather like the absurdist play, *Six Characters in Search of an Author*).

Melinda Kinsman's 2016 book presents the unlikeliest of pairs in *Molly Mouse and the Bear Cub*.

An unlikely friendship can be formed through shared adversity. And one professional picture book author, Mary Hertz Scarbrough, suggests that to create a compelling storyline, you have to get your character in trouble, "To have a great story, you've got to get your main character into trouble . . . How much trouble? It needs to be age-appropriate."

But, she cautions, don't let adults come to the rescue:

> Real kids get told what to do, how to do it, and what not to do *all* the time. Parents, teachers, older siblings, coaches, music instructors—kids have to listen to adults blathering all the livelong day. Think of a child you know and start enumerating how many adults/authority figures that child interacts with on a daily or weekly basis. Sure, a lot of this instruction from one's elders is necessary in real life, but it doesn't make for good literature, not for a young reader, and not if you are the adult reading to a youngster . . . Keep parents and other authority figures in the background (at most); make sure their involvement is minimal. This rule applies even when you're writing for really young kids.
>
> http://www.quickanddirtytips.com/education/writing/
> common-mistakes-to-avoid-when-writing-a-childrens-
> book"oid-when-writing-a-childrens-book#sthash.2ZDDq2Cm.dpuf

The final step:

How does your story end? Happily, of course. But consider also:

- ► What has your character learned?

- ► How is he changed?

- ► How has his empathy for your other character increased and, importantly, expanded to embrace other living creatures?

FEATURE

Look at these images. Then construct a brief plot summary based on a storyline that the images suggest. There is no one "right" answer. Be creative!

©Katelka/Shutterstock.com

©suerz/Shutterstock.com

©GraphicsRF/Shutterstock.com

Lesson

©cs333/Shutterstock.com

Get Anthropomorphic

The first step:

Let me tell you about Lilly. She loves everything about school, from the snacks in the cafeteria to the sounds of her boots on the shiny hallways. She especially loves her teacher, and wants to be just like him when she grows up. He's an unorthodox and enthusiastic teacher, a sharp dresser, with colorful ties and eyeglasses on a chain around his neck. Lilly likes to pretend to be a teacher, giving her baby brother lessons at home.

Now, just based on what you know from the paragraph above, draw a picture of Lilly. (Don't worry; artistic skills are not part of this exercise.)

What does Lilly look like in your drawing? Is she seated at a table in the school cafeteria eating a yummy slice of pizza, or walking down the hall in a pair of trendy boots? Is she at home giving a "lesson" to her baby brother, perhaps standing in front of a homemade chalkboard? In terms of her age, did you envision her to be a teenager, or more likely a young elementary school aged child, perhaps kindergarten, judging from her enthusiasm about school?

Next, draw a picture of her teacher. Again, using only the information provided above to form your impressions of him.

What does the teacher in your drawing look like? Is he old, or young? An "unorthodox" teacher could be at either end of his teaching career. Is he young because Lilly perhaps seems to have a crush on him, or is he more of a father (or grandfather) figure?

Is he . . . a rodent? What! Yes, I said "rodent." If you are familiar with Kevin Henke's much-beloved character Lilly, the star of *Lilly's Purple Plastic Purse* (just published in a twentieth anniversary edition) and its subsequent sequels, such as *Lilly's Big Day* (a *New York Times* Bestseller), then you knew all along that Lilly, and her teacher, her brother, are all mice. But when I read the book aloud to my classes without ever showing the graphics, the students who don't know the book inevitably draw human characters. When I show them the book, they always shout out in surprise, "They're MICE!"

Why is that a surprise? Because they are anthropomorphic characters.

The next step:

Let's define anthropomorphic by breaking the word down:

> anthro = human
>
> morph = to change

This refers to a non-human character, most commonly an animal, who exhibits human qualities.

But it could also be an inanimate object, as in *Pinocchio, Winnie the Pooh*, or *Toy Story*.

What about *Charlotte's Web*? Well, she lives in a web, doesn't she? Whereas Lilly apparently does not live in a mouse nest or fear cats (although she does like to eat cheesy snacks).

To be completely anthropomorphic, the character should exhibit no animal behaviors. But it is common to have an animal with some anthropomorphic qualities, which can be a charming combination. In the 1960s TV show of the same name, Mr. Ed was a talking horse but he lived in a stall and behaved as a horse in every way; it's just that he could talk to his owner, which of course led to many (mis)adventures.

The final step:

Consider incorporating anthropomorphic elements into your animal character. Do this as an exercise, even if you ultimately decide not to keep the ideas in your final draft.

Probably your human character will need to communicate with her friend, so the animal could talk to her in human language, or perhaps through some form of animal language like Curious George with the man in the big yellow hat. Or she could somehow learn to speak "dog" like Dr. Dolittle.

An exotic animal could come into the human house, as in *Hooray for Amanda and Her Alligator*, written and illustrated by Mo Willems.

Or it could be even more fun, imaginative, and empathy invoking to have the human enter into the animal's world, like *Alice in Wonderland*.

Lesson

©cs333/Shutterstock.com

Write the Text

The first step:

As was emphasized in the Introduction to the Picture Book Unit, a good working definition of "Picture Book" is a work of children's literature in which text and graphics are *equally* important. As represented in the equation: Text + Graphics = Meaning.

Creating the text is, therefore, half the battle—or, half the joy—of this project. Some specific considerations regarding the textual component of your book are:

- ▶ Number of words
- ▶ Age-appropriate words
- ▶ Use of first-person vs. third-person narration
- ▶ Dialogue (and, perhaps, dialect)
- ▶ Use of present or past tense (but not both!)

The Introduction to the Unit emphasized the parallel between poetry and picture books: their sparseness of language makes every word carry extra weight. As you write your text, you should consider making use of some poetic devices such as:

- alliteration

- repetition

- imagery

- onomatopoeia

Don't overlook the importance of your title. It is, after all, the first words of your text that your reader will encounter. From these words—in conjunction with your cover graphics—a reader will draw inferences and expectations about the book. However, while they are the first words read, they should probably be the last words written. You will have a better idea of the best title only after the story is written. For now, a working title will suffice.

The next step:

Also, and this is the big one, write the book. Of course, you should do this in equal-parts collaboration with your child, allowing him to suggest the direction. But if your child is reticent to begin, or if he encounters "writer's block" at any point in the process, you should be ready to suggest a direction. Brainstorming could begin with something as mundane as, "What did you and Bozo do this morning?" "Well . . . I fed him." "Okay." "And then we went for a walk . . ." "Good! Where did you go? What did you see there? Who did you meet?" Through these kinds of questions, a typical, even boring, day can turn into an adventure!

Conversely, you may have to rein in your child if his imagination runs away with him. ". . . and then the hippo started to eat the faces off the flowers in the park, and . . . " Whoa! This is an actual example from one of my students. But she gently, and successfully, redirected her child's energy into a less destructive action.

As you write your story, remember that all good plots have twists. Billy and Bozo went to the park and came home is not a very captivating story. If they are abducted by aliens in the park, well, now you have an unexpected plot twist, and an adventure!

A word about words:

A typical picture book, intended for K–2nd graders can have anywhere from ten to 200 words per page. An average book of thirty-two pages could contain 200 to 700 words total. As an example, *Where the Wild Things Are* is less than 400 words. For your ten-page book, you should aim for approximately 300 words.

When it comes to "age appropriate" words, don't be afraid to challenge young readers with unfamiliar words, as long as you follow these two rules:

- Don't use too many (three unfamiliar words in a book of 300 words is enough)

- Be sure to provide "context clues"

A good example of a "context" clue can be found in Kevin Henkes' *Lilly's Purple Plastic Purse*. One caption states that her purse plays a jaunty tune when it's opened. Most young children—and many adults—would be unfamiliar with the word "jaunty," but from the happy illustration of Lilly dancing, it can be surmised that a "jaunty" tune is an upbeat style of music and not a funeral dirge.

In addition to incorporating a few challenging words, you should also strive to be "authentic" in your word choices. This is best done by listening attentively to your child.

One of my students' books included a page that read: "They went to the park and played on the swing, the slide and the spinning thing."

My student explained that her child had used the expression "spinning thing" because she didn't know the word "merry-go-round." My student made the right decision to not "correct" the child's language. "Spinning thing" was perfect because it was authentic.

The final step:

Now that your text is completed, you need to PROOFREAD!!!!

In children's literature, there is zero tolerance for misspelled words, incorrect punctuation, or any kind of grammatical error. After all, your child will be learning these mistakes. Look at the following examples; is there anything incorrect?

> Billy walked his dog in the park. He sees another dog. That dog was big!

Did you notice the shift in tenses? This can be avoided by remaining consistent in either present or past tense.

Present Tense:

> Billy is walking his dog. He sees another dog. That dog is big!

Past Tense:

> Billy walked his dog in the park. He saw another dog. That dog was big!

A good way to catch tense shifts is by reading your book aloud. This is something you should do anyway to be sure that you have created a good read-aloud book.

FEATURE

©nataka/Shutterstock.com

©nataka/Shutterstock.com

©Bannykh Alexey Vladimirovh/Shutterstock.com

Write a series of three-sentence captions for these illustrations.

> ► First person

> ► Third person

> ► Present tense

> ► Past tense

Consider also the tone of each image. Did your text accurately reflect the mood that the image seems to convey?

Lesson

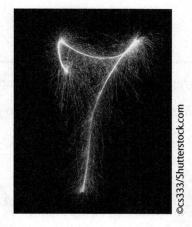

©cs333/Shutterstock.com

Create the Illustrations

The first step:

You may not be an artist, but every child is artistic! Consider inviting your child to create at least some illustrations that could be incorporated into the graphic layout of your book. Some is better than none, and it's also better than all. When a picture book is composed entirely of children's original drawings, it is almost always very difficult to reproduce and ends up looking faint or sloppy. On the other hand, it is a nice, personal touch to have a few original drawings as key elements incorporated into some of the pages.

The next step:

Make use of book-making software such as Storyjumper, Mystorybook, or Blurb Book. You may also use PowerPoint, although it will be a more complicated process to print the physical book with this software, whereas Storyjumper will create the book for you (for a price).

Through your graphics, as with your text, you want to create empathy. The tone of your illustrations should match the tone of your text.

Pamela Zagarenski's cover illustration for the 2012 Caldecott medalist *Sleep Like a Tiger* shows a peaceful tiger sleeping soundly, with a tiny ragdoll in its paw, and author Mary Logue's not-sleepy protagonist tucked in safely beside the animal. What if the cover instead showed a more realistic tiger stalking its prey in a jungle setting? Would that be the appropriate tone for this book? Of course not.

FEATURE

Look at these two examples. Which graphic captures the appropriate tone to match the caption?

Leon the lion is hoping that you will come out to play with him.

©Teguh Mujiono/Shutterstock.com

©Memo Angeles/Shutterstock.com

The final step:

After you've created the illustrations for all of your interior pages, it's finally time to design your cover. What: design the cover last? Just as your final title likely changed after the full text was completed, you probably have a better idea on the best cover for your book after the interior pages are done. You may incorporate some elements from an interior page for your cover, but avoid simply using an interior page *as* your cover. On the back cover, include a photo of you and your child working together, with a statement acknowledging his contribution.

Lesson

©cs333/Shutterstock.com

Design the Pages

The first step:

Take a look again at the picture book you said was your favorite. If you can't put your finger on a copy readily, look it up on Amazon or the library's online catalog. Is there one name listed as author/illustrator, or are there separate names for author and illustrator? The latter is more common in the picture book industry. In that case, the author is responsible for deciding where the page breaks occur by submitting his or her text broken up into ten (or more) separate pages. Now it's time for you to do the same. Consider where a page break should come in terms of the progression of the story or perhaps at a key turning point.

The next step:

You should also:

- ▶ Vary the amount of text on a page

- ▶ For emphasis, try one page with just one word on it

- ▶ Think in terms of a double-page spread, where appropriate

In one of my students' books, the story told of a gorilla displaced by a forest fire that destroyed his home. Over the next four pages, he

      Travelled

            And travelled

                  And travelled

                          Until at last he found a new home.

On each page, the illustrations showed a different kind of environment that the gorilla was travelling across, from desert to forest to ice caps in the ocean. Together, these sparse words and diverse illustrations presented the idea of far-flung travel and the passage of time as well as the crossing of space.

The final step:

Consider the last page. Does it emphasize the theme of empathy for our fellow creatures? Does the illustration show your child happily hugging his new best friend, and does the text celebrate their bonding and their successful overcoming of obstacles in their adventure?

Perhaps there is even a suggestion of the next adventure to come?

Lesson

©cs333/Shutterstock.com

Research and Reflect

The first step:

A good teacher is always reflecting on the classroom experience, through both informal and formal assessment.

> What worked well?
>
> What surprised you?
>
> What would you do differently?
>
> What do you think your students learned?

Did your students learn what you had intended; in other words, did you meet your objective?

Therefore, each of our four units will involve a short written reflection as a summative experience.

The next step:

After creating the picture book project, compose a thesis-driven 1,000-word essay incorporating outside research with your own reflection on the experience.

The bibliography listed at the end of this book contains a number of reliable outside sources, or you may prefer to consult the library or check additional online Web sites.

You may, if you wish, include quotations from one or more picture books, including your own, but these are "primary texts" and do not count as "research" material.

The standard five-paragraph theme format is useful for such a short paper:

> ► State your thesis
>
> ► Support it with a brief quotation from one or two outside sources
>
> ► Briefly describe what you did in the picture book project . . .
>
> ► . . . and what you learned
>
> ► Restate your thesis indicating that it is supported by your research and firsthand experience

Yes, it is permissible—even desirable—in a reflection essay to use the first person ("I").

Keep in mind that a thesis is not just a topic sentence: "This essay is about picture books." It contains both the topic and an opinion: "Picture books are important in a child's development."

For this project, a possible thesis might be: "Picture books can be used to inspire empathy for all living creatures." It could be supported by your child's newfound appreciation for a type of animal she did not like before.

Another possible thesis might be: "Picture books can develop a child's imagination." It might be supported by examples of especially inventive ideas in your child's story.

The final step:

After drafting your essay, be sure that you have included proper citations for any quoted or paraphrased materials, following MLA citation format. The Purdue University Web site is a helpful resource for MLA format questions:

https://owl.english.purdue.edu/owl/resource/747/01/

Finally, proofread carefully for spelling, grammar, or punctuation errors.

Lesson

©cs333/Shutterstock.com

Prepare to Teach

The first step:

In the project that you completed for this unit, you worked with just one child and created just one picture book. When you begin teaching, you will need to expand this project into a full week-long unit plan.

Your unit plan should open with a context statement or rationale for the unit. Before describing what you will do each day, step back and think about WHY you are presenting a unit like this. Why do you think it is valuable for your students to spend a week reading, studying, and creating picture books? And, in particular, why is it beneficial for them to be working with animals or plants as characters in their book?

Assume that you will devote one class hour to the lesson on each day. Then design the specific activities, along with your objectives or goals for what you hope your students will learn each day.

Be careful not to confuse "objective" with "activity."

"Read a picture book."—This is an activity, something you will *do* with your students in this lesson.

"Understand how pictures and text work together."—This is an objective, something you want your students to *learn* through the lesson.

The next step:

Design a daily lesson plan template that works for you. You can get ideas from Web sites or education manuals, but ultimately it is a matter of individual preference. Some essential categories to include are:

- ▶ objectives
- ▶ materials needed
- ▶ activities
- ▶ assessments

Whether you list them in this order or a different order, whether you put the information in boxes or columns, and whether the information is expressed in complete sentences or fragments in a bulleted list, all of this is up to your personal discretion.

A sample lesson plan is provided on the following page.

The final step:

Connect to core standards, as applicable in your state. You should consult the Department of Education Web site for current standards for your state. For example:

http://www.doe.in.gov/standards/englishlanguage-arts

Lesson Plan: Day One

Lesson Topic	Introduction to Picture Books and Picture Book Unit
Objectives	To get students started on the unit with thorough understanding of the assignment and sample materials
Materials Needed	Daily PowerPoint (on Blackboard) *Brave Potatoes* (Web link) *Where Once There Was a Wood* (book)
Activities	*Introductory activities:* Take attendance Create a seating chart Circulate picture book selection sheet *New information:* Review the assignment information in the syllabus and rubric posted on our Blackboard site Brainstorm a working definition of "picture book" Show the video of *Brave Potatoes* (6 minutes) Discuss the concept of "cross-generational appeal" using examples from the book Read *Where Once There Was a Wood* Pre-reading: Choose a "woods" animal During reading: Raise a hand if "your" animal is mentioned Post-reading: Which animals were not mentioned; create a page for them *Closing activities:* Brief review of the day's main points Invite questions Next class: concept of "age appropriateness"
Assessment	Informal assessment: asking for questions from the class throughout the lesson, as well as a brief summary at the end
Standards Addressed	

NAME _____

This sheet MUST be submitted during your presentation!

	Poor	**Satisfactory**	**Outstanding**

OVERALL:

Effectively addresses theme

THE BOOK:

Attractive cover page

Attractive pages

Appropriate text

NO misspelled words

PRESENTATION:

Clear and articulate

GRADE: _____

Unit Two

Fairy Tales

(Grades 3–4)

©Hibrida/Shutterstock.com

Introduction

> For a story to hold the child's attention, it must entertain him and arouse his curiosity. But to enrich his life, it must stimulate his imagination; help him to develop his intellect and to clarify his emotions; be attuned to his anxieties and aspirations; give full recognition to his difficulties, while at the same time suggesting solutions to the problems which perturb him. In short, it must at one and the same time relate to all aspects of his personality— and this without ever belittling, but, on the contrary, giving full credence to the serious- ness of the child's predicaments, while simultaneously promoting confidence in himself.
> —Bruno Bettelheim, *The Uses of Enchantment*

Whew! Can fairy tales do all that? Can any genre of literature do all that?

A leading child psychologist and defender of fairy tales, Bettelheim believes that these archaic and often arcane archetypal stories are uniquely able to connect to children and inspire them to be heroes in their own stories.

> Today children no longer grow up within the security of an extended family, or of a well-integrated community. Therefore, even more than at the times fairy tales were invented, it is important to provide the modern child with images of heroes who have to go out into the world all by themselves and who, although originally ignorant of the ultimate things, find secure places in the world by following their right way with deep inner confidence.
> Bruno Bettelheim, *The Uses of Enchantment*

It is important to keep in mind that fairy tales did not originate with Walt Disney. Nor even with the Grimm Brothers. People have been telling each other fairy tales since ancient times. A very significant literature genre, fairy tales are present in all cultures around the world. It wasn't until the seventeenth century that fairy tales in Europe were written down and published.

Originally, folk tales and fairy tales were intended for adult audiences. As such, it is common to find in early versions of beloved tales such as *Little Red Riding Hood* or *Cinderella* overt references to graphic violence and even sexual activity. For an adult audience, this would have been acceptable, even desir- able, but when such tales were adapted by Disney these adult themes were removed and replaced by adorable singing mice.

(For the differences between these two terms often used interchangeably—folk tales and fairy tales—see Lesson 3.)

While elements such as those mentioned above may make folk tales seem inappropriate for children, other elements make them very appropriate. The adults for whom they were created had much in com- mon with children. Working-class peasants were minimally literate, so simple language, single plots, and stock characters were often employed. This, coupled with devices such as repetition, also made the tales easier to recite orally, and each storyteller could add his or her own embellishments and variations. This ultimately led to the countless variants found today.

Furthermore, these hardworking adults enjoyed stories where the little guy is victorious over the bigger, more powerful, tyrant. To them, this represented their struggles against their employers, or slave masters, whereas for children they might represent parents or teachers or other adults before whom they too feel powerless. They delight to see the weaker outwit the stronger, the little beat the bigger.

Think of:

- ▶ Jack in the beanstalk outwitting the giant

- ▶ Hansel and Gretel overcoming the witch

- ▶ Puss in Boots conquering the ogre

If fairy tales are beneficial to children in so many ways, why would some parents oppose the use of fairy tales in their children's classroom? Take a minute and consider a possible opposing viewpoint before reading on.

Okay, what arguments did you consider?

The most prominent argument is that the traditional fairy tale ending is unrealistic. Most of us do not meet our Prince Charming and live "happily ever after." Others object to the use of magic and other forms of fantasy, which come to the aid of every damsel in distress. And the gender roles are sometimes seen as negatively stereotypical.

Even if you don't agree with these arguments, it's important to be aware of them, recognize them, and be prepared with a counter argument of your own. Or you may quote Bettelheim, who concludes that "fairy tales have unequaled value, because they offer new dimensions to the child's imagination which would be impossible for him to discover as truly on his own. Even more important, the form and structure of fairy tales suggest images to the child by which he can structure his daydreams and with them give better direction to his life."

The Project

Introduce your students to diverse cultures through international fairy tales.

Lesson One: Choose a Country

Lesson Two: Choose a Tale

Lesson Three: Types of Tales

Lesson Four: Universality in Tales

Lesson Five: Diversity in Tales

Lesson Six: Research Your Country

Lesson Seven: Children in Your Country

Lesson Eight: Present Your Tale

Lesson Nine: Research and Reflect

Lesson Ten: Prepare to Teach

Lesson

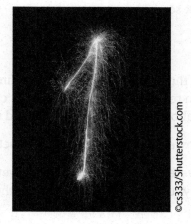

©cs333/Shutterstock.com

Choose a Country

The first step:

No matter if you and your students are in a small town in Middle America, this unit allows you to introduce them to the world! Most of your children will not have travelled out of the country, and many never will, so this unit is an important opportunity to introduce them to the world's wonderful diversity.

Start by considering, where in the world would *you* like to go? Name three countries, in order of preference.

The next step:

Consider the reasons for your choice.

Was it:

- ▶ someplace where you went on spring break?
- ▶ the land of your ancestors?
- ▶ a language you studied in high school?

These are all legitimate reasons for you to be interested in a given country, but are they reasons for your students to be interested? One female student chose the Caribbean islands for her unit, because in her words, "the men there are hot!" Can you envision her standing before a group of eight-year-olds, introducing her fairy tale unit by stating, "Class, we will be travelling to the Caribbean this week because the men there are hot"? No, I didn't think so.

The final step:

Go back now and look at your list of three. What would children find of interest in each country? After you've brainstormed, and maybe even researched a bit, you should choose the one country of your three that children would be most excited about. This is why you needed to have three options.

Think about popular TV shows or movies. Is there a show that is set in one of your countries?

Finally, try to recall places that you were interested in when you were a child. Those same places might be interesting to children today. And you might enjoy "revisiting" them as an adult.

Lesson

©cs333/Shutterstock.com

Choose a Tale

The first step:

Now that you have your country selected, it is an easy step to locate tales from the country. If you chose Armenia, for example, simply Google the following set of keywords: Armenian folktales or folk tales of Armenia. If you know that you want a particular type of tale, you can narrow your search somewhat by using keywords such as: Armenian fairy tales or Armenian fables. You should also consult the excellent Web site worldoftales.com. You might even consider searching the library, where you will find many picture book editions of fairy tales.

The next step:

Finding tales from your country is the easy step; choosing which one to use is more difficult. Consider the pros and cons of choosing a familiar tale. According to worldoftales.com, the following are some of the most popular fairy tales. See how many of them you already know:

Cinderella

Sleeping Beauty

Little Tom Thumb

Rumpelstiltskin

The Ugly Duckling

Puss in Boots

Little Red Riding Hood

Beauty and the Beast

The Little Mermaid

The Princess and the Pea

What do you think might be a negative aspect of choosing a familiar tale? On the other hand, can you also think of a positive one?

Let's consider the negative first. If your students (or your classmates) are already familiar with the tale itself, you risk boring them with your presentation. Wouldn't you be tempted to doze off during a presentation that informed you that *Little Red Riding Hood* is a story about a little girl who takes a basket of goodies to her Grandmother and on the way to her house she meets a wolf who. . . . Hey, wake up! You get the idea; simply telling students a story they already know is not very engaging—or educational.

On the other hand, if you begin with the recognition that they already know the story, you do have a nice platform from which to introduce an international variant of the tale, indicating those examples of diversity as discussed in Lesson 4. You will also then be able to connect some of those "diverse" details of the tale with some details about the country itself.

For example, if you found a variant of the Little Red story that came from an island nation, where the wicked wolf might be portrayed as a malevolent sea creature, you could teach your students about the importance of the sea to that culture.

There are pros and cons also to selecting a less familiar tale from a less familiar culture. In this case, you will need to spend a good deal more time presenting the story itself, at the risk of not spending enough time on the country. Some examples of less familiar tales would be:

> **Tanzania:** *The Ape, the Snake, and the Lion*
>
> **India:** *The Magic Pitcher*
>
> **Australia:** *The Galah, and Oolah the Lizard*
>
> **South Africa:** *Lion and Jackal*

The final step:

One final word of caution: be sure that the tale you pick is, in fact, a folk tale. As discussed in the next lesson, the essential definition of "folk tale" is a tale that has been passed down for generations or even centuries with no known author.

Then, consider the following; do they fit the definition?

> *Alice's Adventures in Wonderland*
>
> *The Wizard of Oz*
>
> *Peter Pan*

Why not? Because, although each story can be considered a "classic" among children's literature, each one is a book that has a known author: Lewis Carroll, L. Frank Baum, and J.M. Barrie, respectively.

Trickster Tales

©spawn101/Shutterstock.com

Trickster tales are beloved by children because they present a small or weak character outwitting a large or strong one. One of the most famous of tricksters in folk tales is Anansi.

Anansi is a West African god in the form of a spider. He is cunning and tricky, and uses his cunning guile to try to get what he wants. Anansi was originally found in stories from the Ashanti people in Ghana, and from there the stories spread through West Africa. During the Atlantic slave trade, the stories crossed the ocean with the slaves through oral tradition.

Anansi shares similarities with the African-American trickster Br'er Rabbit, who originated from the folk-lore of south and central Africa. Like the Anansi stories, they depict a physically small and vulnerable creature using his cunning intelligence to prevail over larger animals.

During the time of the African slave trade, Anansi's cunning ways symbolized a resistance to powerful slave owners.

Some Anansi tales are:

>   *Anansi Tries to Steal All the Wisdom in the World*
>
>   *Anansi and the Pot of Beans*
>
>   *Anansi and Turtle Go to Dinner*

FEATURE

Pourquois Tales

©file404/Shutterstock.com

Pourquois is the French word for "why"—a favorite word for children.

Some pourquois tales, such as Kipling's famous *Just So Stories*, explain how something came to be. Like a myth, the Pourquois tale provides a supernatural explanation of the creation or alteration of a natural phenomenon or animal.

When Ms. Frizzle in *The Magic School Bus* series (Scholastic) takes her students through the use of fantasy inside the human body, she does so to explain how it works with scientific accuracy.

Conversely, pourquois tales are "entertaining lies"; they explain a scientific phenomenon—such as why the sky is blue—in an entertaining, and scientifically inaccurate, way.

Although the word "pourquois" is French, pourquois tales can be found around the world. Some examples are:

> ▶ *Why the Bat Flies by Night*—from Nigeria
>
> ▶ *Why Dogs Chase Cats*—from Malaysia
>
> ▶ *The Story of the Milky Way*—from the Cherokee people

Lesson

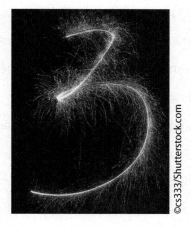

©cs333/Shutterstock.com

Types of Tales

The first step:

Now that you have already spent some time searching for tales from your country, it's time to step back and consider the distinction between two terms that are often used almost interchangeably, although they do have different definitions: folk tales and fairy tales.

"Folk tale" is the umbrella category, under which "fairy" is one type of tale.

> ► *All fairy tales are folk tales, but not all folk tales are fairy tales.*

To use another example: All Volkswagens are cars, but not all cars are Volkswagens. Make sense?

The example of Volkswagen also gives us a chance to consider the term folk tale. "Volk" in German translates as folk, or the common people. Folk tales are tales that were intended for the "volk," the common people.

The next step:

Folklorist Stith Thompson classifies the tales into countless categories, but for our purposes, we'll focus on the most common types among the tales adapted for children:

- ► Fairy—unspecified time and place; always includes a magical element
- ► Trickster—features a clever character overcoming others through his wit
- ► Animal—main character is an animal; may or may not be anthropomorphic
- ► Fable—end with the moral explicitly stated
- ► Simpleton—features a dim-witted but sympathetic character
- ► Legend—purports to be a "true" story
- ► Myth—deals with gods and/or goddesses
- ► Pourquois—a humorous explanation for some natural phenomenon

Fairy is by far the most prevalent tale type, and the one you are most likely to choose for your project. In comparison to myths and legends, the time and place of occurrence in fairy tales is vague: "Once upon a time in a land far far away. . . ." The characteristics of fairy tales include the appearance of fantastic elements in the form of talking animals, magic, witches, giants, knights, and heroes.

The final step:

You'll need to be able to identify which category your chosen tale falls under, but it's important to keep in mind that most tales overlap two or more of these categories. For example, a tale may feature animal characters that are tricksters and/or simpletons. A fairy tale may end with an explicit moral, placing it also in the fable category.

Lesson

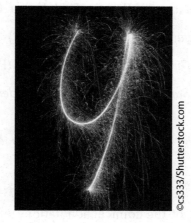

Universality in Tales

The first step:

In presenting fairy tales to your students, you want to emphasize both the tale's universality (the ways in which it is similar to tales with which they are familiar) and diversity (the ways in which it is different, unique to the country of its origin).

Let's start with a tale that is familiar to all of us, *Cinderella*, and look at the way it is both the same and different in a number of cultural variants.

> The story of Cinderella, perhaps the best-known fairy tale, is told or read to children of very young ages. But Cinderella is not just one story; more than 500 versions have been found—just in Europe! The tale's origins appear to date back to a Chinese story from the ninth century, 'Yeh-Shen.' Almost every culture seems to have its own version, and every storyteller his or her tale.
>
> —http://www.ala.org/offices/resources/multicultural

The next step:

Read several versions of the story through the many multicultural adaptations that are readily available. Here are some examples:

Climo, Shirley. *The Egyptian Cinderella*. Illus. by Ruth Heller. (HarperCollins, 1989)

Steptoe, John. *Mufaro's Beautiful Daughters*. (Lothrop, 1987)

Martin, Rafe. *The Rough-Face Girl*. Illus. by David Shannon (Putnam, 1992)

Hickox, Rebecca. *The Golden Sandal: A Middle Eastern Cinderella Story*. Illus. by Will Hillenbrand. (Holiday, 1998)

Jaffe, Nina. *The Way Meat Loves Salt: A Cinderella Tale from the Jewish Tradition*. Illus. by Louise August. (Holt, 1998)

Louie, Ai-Ling. *Yeh-Shen: A Cinderella Story from China*. Illus. by Ed Young. (Putnam, 1982)

Just for fun, you might also enjoy one of the comical adaptations such as:

The Irish "Cinderlad" by Shirley Climo and Loretta Krupinksi (Trophy Books, 2000)

Smoky Mountain Rose: The Appalachian Cinderella, by Alan Schroeder and Brad Sneed (Puffin, 2000)

Bubba the Cowboy Prince: A Fractured Texas Tale, by Helen Ketterman; Illus. by James Warhola. (Scholastic, 1997)

Make a list of similarities to the version, perhaps by Disney, with which you are most familiar. What are some of the essential ingredients that tell you it is a Cinderella story?

▶ A good protagonist (usually, but not always, a young woman)

▶ An evil antagonist (usually a mean step-mother)

▶ Jealous step-siblings (usually two sisters)

▶ A supernatural aide (some sort of "fairy godmother" figure)

▶ And, of course, the "handsome prince"

▶ But for our protagonist to be saved by him requires a "shoe" test

This is a common motif in folk tales, as noted by folklorist Stith Thompson. *Archetypes and Motifs in Folklore and Literature* (M.E. Sharpe, 2005), edited by Jane Garry and Hasan el-Shamy, includes a discussion of the sexual symbolism of the shoe in many folk and fairy tales, adding that "any such symbolic value would be lost on younger listeners, but not on older members of the storyteller's audience." This attests to the "multiple levels of significance contained in most of the stories" (238).

The final step:

What conclusions can we draw about the ways in which we are all "universal"? What values, emotions, or circumstances do we share with others around the world?

Lesson

©cs333/Shutterstock.com

Diversity in Tales

The first step:

We've already noted that in presenting fairy tales to your students, you want to emphasize both the tale's universality (the ways in which it is similar to tales with which they are familiar) and diversity (the ways in which it is different, unique to the country of its origin).

In the previous lesson, you took a tale that is familiar to all of us and looked at the way it is the same as the Cinderella we know and love. Now, let's look at how some of the story is different in some of the multicultural variants.

The next step:

Make a list of the differences that are unique to the country of its origin. Taking just one example—the fairy godmother—we can see how malleable the tale is and how this one variant reflects the culture of the tale's origin:

- ▶ In Egypt: a falcon
- ▶ In Ireland: a cow
- ▶ In China: a fish
- ▶ In Appalachia: a pig

The final step:

Details such as those listed above suggest that animals were more often seen as a source of magical aide than human figures. The pig and cow in two of the tales further reflect the agricultural nature of the region.

To draw an even more significant inference about a culture through reading their version of the tale, let's look at the Algonquin variant, *The Rough-Faced Girl*.

In this version, the Cinderella character does not attract her Prince Charming through external beauty, such as a ballroom gown; nor does their encounter take place in a public venue. Instead, she is recognized for her good heart; her "beauty" is within.

Lesson

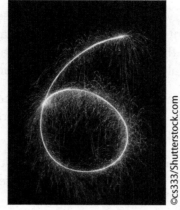

©cs333/Shutterstock.com

Research Your Country

The first step:

A fun way to approach the research component of this project is to imagine that you are planning to go on vacation to the country you chose. Better yet, imagine that you will be taking your class on a school trip there. That way, you will be looking for places and activities that they may find most interesting.

A useful Web site is Marie's Pastiche Exploring World Cultures with Kids: http://www.mariespastiche.com.

Click on the link to "Games from Around the World." Here you'll find the Italian lawn game of Bocce, the West African board game Derrah, Queah & Oware, Chinese tangram puzzles, and more. It's one way to get to know a country from a child's perspective.

The next step:

On the Internet, you can also find some practical information that you would need for your trip, such as: How long will your flight take? How much will it cost? Where will you have to change planes along the way?

What does the country look like? Is it mountainous or flat? Surrounded by water, or by land? These are connections you should make to the tale you chose.

What is unique about the country? Unusual animals, landmarks, or cultural practices such as festivals? These may connect to your tale, as well, and will certainly provide excitement for your students.

The final step:

A research project on a foreign country too often suggests the need to focus on the country's history; but your children will be much more interested in the country today. Keep your focus on what they will experience in their visit, and the way that children live there today. Don't worry about the year of its independence, the names of its political leaders, or the gross national product of its economy.

Instead, look for "fun facts" that you can share, and make them come alive for your children. Did you know that in Japan there are eight cats to every one person? If your class is comprised of twenty-five students, you can tell them to imagine 200 cats in their classroom!

Going to Australia to feed a kangaroo or pet a koala is more exciting to the average eight-year-old than learning about the continent's origin as a penal colony in the eighteenth century.

Lesson

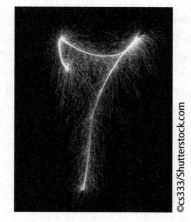

©cs333/Shutterstock.com

Children in Your Country

The first step:

An excellent resource for learning about the typical day in the life for children around the world is the Web site: http://www.timeforkids.com. From the home page, click on "Around the World," and then choose a region of the world. For example, Japan. Once in the site for Japan, click on "Day in the Life," and you will meet Ryuichi through a smiling photograph and personal welcome statement in which he tells us that he is ten years old and lives with his parents, grandparents, and sisters outside of Tokyo. "Read how I spend a typical day," he invites us.

Clicking on the alarm clock icons from 6:00 a.m. through 7:00 p.m., we learn that Ryuichi has rice and fish for breakfast, loves math in school, and plays video games before sitting down to supper with his family.

The next step:

As with your tale, here too, you are looking to highlight universals first and foremost, followed by some examples of diversity. Because you want to promote the kind of compassion for other cultures that you inspired for animals in your picture book project, you don't want to begin by emphasizing how these children are different, strange, or in any way unsympathetic. Start with what they have in common with your students. Their day includes breakfast, going to school, playing games or sports.

What's different is what they have for breakfast; what their school day is like; what games or sports they play?

Even greater differences may be evident in countries that are much poorer that our own. This may inspire a class project to try to raise some money for children through a charitable organization such as the Save the Children Fund, commonly known as Save the Children, which is an international non-governmental organization that promotes children's rights, provides relief and helps support children in developing countries. Established in the United Kingdom in 1919, it seeks to "improve the lives of children through better education, health care, and economic opportunities, as well as providing emergency aid in natural disasters, war, and other conflicts.

—http://www.savethechildren.org.

The final step:

Introduce your children to one or more children from the country—literally. This could be done in a number of ways:

▶ Class visit

  Invite a foreign exchange student or a student with parents/grandparents from the country, or a teacher who has been to the country and can talk about school in that area.

▶ Skype or Facetime

  Technology makes such exciting classroom experiences possible, but keep in mind the time differences involved. Your 8:00 a.m. class might be in the middle of the night for children in Africa.

▶ Email pen pals

  Having pen pals with children in a distant country is also much easier through the use of technology. You don't have to wait for weeks to receive a reply to your letter, but because of the time differences noted above, you may have to wait until the following class day.

Lesson

©cs333/Shutterstock.com

Present Your Tale

The first step:

To really bring this unit to life, you will need to create a PowerPoint or Prezi presentation for your students, introducing them to all of the elements of this unit: the country, its children, and the tale.

Let's review the elements of a good presentation:

- ► engaging graphics
- ► animation
- ► music or sound effects
- ► sparse text

And, no misspelled words! There is nothing worse than putting a slide up on the big screen that says,

> *Welcome to Itly!*

Therefore, you must proofread carefully, and you should also practice the presentation aloud.

The next step:

Choosing graphics. The first slide should be a grabber! It should convey the exciting idea that you will be "travelling" to a distant and exotic land. Ethnically appropriate music is a nice touch, or a short clip of dancers in ethnic costume. Unusual animals or landscapes are other good possibilities. Perhaps the colorful flag of the nation.

As an extra touch to the idea of travel, for this unit you could have your students create their own "passport" where you could insert a stamp for each country they visit.

Whether it is your first or second slide, you should present a world map. Ask your students if they can locate the country on the map. Start with something easier by asking them first to locate where they are on the map. Then, once they, or you, locate the country they are traveling to, you can give them an idea of the distance from here to there.

- ► How many miles

- ► How many hours

- ► How many episodes of Sponge Bob

A fun touch is to have a clip-art airplane fly across the world map, from home to destination.

A second map could zoom in on the country itself. A topographical map could give a sense of the terrain: Is it a mountainous land or an island surrounded by water?

The final step:

Next, one or more slides could show several glimpses of the country itself. Here again you should select elements that would appeal to your children more than to you. For example, one of my students in his presentation on Spain included photos of flamenco dancers and flaming shots of whiskey. Another student, in her presentation on Japan, included photos of an amusement park and the Tokyo McDonalds. Which do you think was more appropriate?

FEATURE

Around the world, there are many tales addressing how the zebra got its stripes, and in Africa one of the most well-known comes from the native people of the Namibian Kalahari Desert. Many African tales are pourquois tales, dealing with the wild animals and "explaining" their unique look. For example, see http://www.gateway-africa.com/stories/How_the_Zebra_Got_his_Stripes_San.html

Start by reading my version of the tale, below:

> How did the Zebra get his stripes?
>
> Long ago, in Africa, the weather was very hot, with very little water in just a few pools and pans. One of these water pools was guarded by a baboon who did not allow anyone to drink at "his" pool.
>
> One day, a zebra and his son came down to have a drink of water, but the baboon, who was sitting by his fire next to the waterhole, jumped up and barked in a loud voice: "If you want some of my water, you'll have to fight for it!"
>
> Back and forth they went fighting, raising a huge cloud of dust. With a mighty kick, the zebra sent the baboon flying high up among the rocks of the cliff behind them. The baboon landed with a smack on his seat, taking all the hair clean off, and to this very day, he still carries the bare patch where he landed.
>
> Then, the zebra, not looking where he was going, staggered back through the baboon's fire, which scorched him, leaving black burn stripes across his white fur. This sent the zebra galloping away to the savannah plains, where he has stayed ever since.
>
> The baboon and his descendants, however, remain high up among the rocks where they bark defiantly at all strangers, and when they walk around, they still hold up their tails to ease the smarting rock-burn of their bald patched bottoms.

Remember that Africa is not a country but a continent comprised of many countries. A quick check with Wikitravel informs us that Namibia is located in Southern Africa, bordering South Africa, Botswana, Angola, Zambia and the Atlantic Ocean. Formerly a colony of Germany, Namibia gained independence in 1990. Natural attractions include the Namib desert, the Kalahari desert and the world's highest quality diamonds.—http://wikitravel.org/en/Namibia

Which of these graphics are most appropriate for a presentation on this tale and this nation? In each set of five, rank them in order from one through five and briefly state your reason for each ranking.

THE COUNTRY

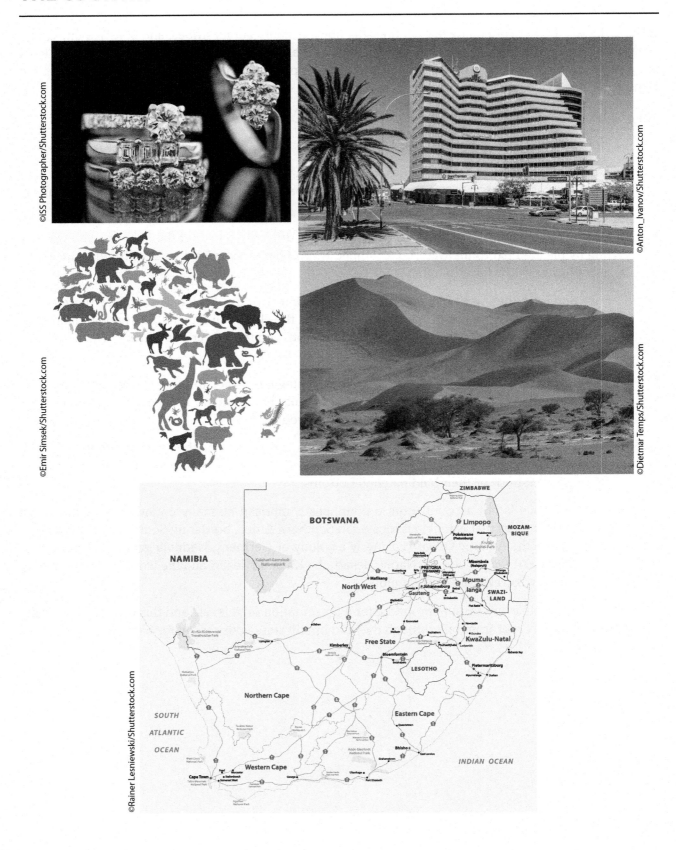

THE CHILDREN

THE TALE

©Andre Valadao/Shutterstock.com

©Ingus Kruklitis/Shutterstock.com

©Prazis/Shutterstock.com

©verzellenberg/Shutterstock.com

©tanapong bhukaswan/Shutterstock.com

Lesson

©cs333/Shutterstock.com

Research and Reflect

The first step:

A good teacher is always reflecting on the classroom experience, through both informal and formal assessment.

> ► What worked well?

> ► What surprised you?

> ► What would you do differently?

> ► What do you think your students learned?

> ► Did your students learn what you had intended; in other words, did you meet your objective?

Therefore, each of our four units will involve a short written reflection as a summative experience.

The next step:

After completing the fairy tale project, compose a thesis-driven 1,000-word essay incorporating outside research with your own reflection on the experience.

The bibliography listed at the end of this book contains a number of reliable outside sources, or you may prefer to consult the library or check additional online Web sites.

You may, if you wish, include quotations from one or more fairy tales, including your own, but these are "primary texts" and do not count as "research" material.

The standard five-paragraph theme format is useful for such a short paper:

> ► State your thesis
>
> ► Support it with a brief quotation from one or two outside sources
>
> ► Briefly describe what you did in the picture book project. . . .
>
> ► . . . and what you learned
>
> ► Restate your thesis indicating that it is supported by your research and firsthand experience

Yes, it is permissible—even even desirable—in a reflection essay to use the first person ("I").

Keep in mind that a thesis is not just a topic sentence: "This essay is about fairy tales." It contains both the topic and an opinion: "Fairy tales are an important form of literature."

For this project, a possible thesis might be: "Fairy tales can be used to inspire empathy for other cultures." It could be supported by your child's newfound appreciation for a country she did not know about before.

The final step:

After drafting your essay, be sure that you have included proper citations for any quoted or paraphrased materials, following MLA citation format. The Purdue University Web site is a helpful resource for MLA format questions:

> https://owl.english.purdue.edu/owl/resource/747/01/

Finally, proofread carefully for spelling, grammar, or punctuation errors.

Lesson

©cs333/Shutterstock.com

Prepare to Teach

The first step:

In the project that you completed for this unit, you worked with just one country and just one tale. When you begin teaching, you will need to expand this project into a full week-long unit plan—with a different country and tale for each day.

Your unit plan should open with a context statement or rationale for the unit. Before describing what you will do each day, step back and think about WHY you are presenting a unit like this. Why do you think it is valuable for your students to spend a week reading and studying folk or fairy tales? And, in particular, why is it beneficial for them to be working with tales from around the world?

Assume that you will devote one class hour to the lesson on each day. Then design the specific activities, along with your objectives or goals for what you hope your students will learn each day.

Be careful not to confuse "objective" with "activity."

> "Read a fairy tale."
> > —This is an activity, something you will *do* with your students in this lesson.

> "Understand how international folk tales reflect the cultures of their origin."
> > —This is an objective, something you want your students to *learn* through the lesson.

The next step:

Design a daily lesson plan template that works for you. You can get ideas from Web sites or education manuals, but ultimately it is a matter of individual preference. Some essential categories to include are:

- ► objectives
- ► materials needed
- ► activities
- ► assessments

But whether you list them in this order or a different order, whether you put the information in boxes or columns, and whether the information is expressed in complete sentences or fragments in a bulleted list. All of this is up to your personal discretion.

A sample lesson plan is provided on the following page.

The final step:

Connect to core standards, as applicable in your state. You should consult the Department of Education Web site for current standards for your state. For example:

http://www.doe.in.gov/standards/englishlanguage-arts

Evaluation Sheet

NAME _____

This sheet MUST be submitted during your presentation!

	Poor	**Satisfactory**	**Outstanding**

OVERALL:

Effectively addresses theme

THE BOOK:

Presents the tale clearly

Presents the country

Engaging graphics

NO misspelled words

PRESENTATION:

Clear and articulate

GRADE: _____

Unit Three

Children's Theater

(Grades 5–6)

©Kilroy79/Shutterstock.com

Introduction

> Alice was beginning to get very tired of sitting by her sister on the bank, and of having nothing to do...when suddenly a White Rabbit with pink eyes ran close by her. There was nothing so very remarkable in that; nor did Alice think it so very much out of the way to hear the Rabbit say to itself, 'Oh dear! Oh dear! I shall be late!' (when she thought it over afterwards, it occurred to her that she ought to have wondered at this, but at the time it all seemed quite natural); but when the Rabbit actually took a watch out of its waistcoat-pocket, and looked at it, and then hurried on, Alice started to her feet, for it flashed across her mind that she had never before seen a rabbit with either a waistcoat-pocket, or a watch to take out of it, and burning with curiosity, she ran across the field after it, and fortunately was just in time to see it pop down a large rabbit-hole under the hedge. In another moment down went Alice after it, never once considering how in the world she was to get out again.
>
> —*Alice's Adventures in Wonderland*, Lewis Carroll (1865)

1865 marks an important date in the history of children's literature. Before the eighteenth century, there was no separate genre of literature for children, and throughout most of the nineteenth century, literature that was written for children was "didactic," intended to teach a lesson. That lesson could be in morals or in foreign language, as in the earliest known picture book: *Orbis Sensualium Pictus*. published in Latin in 1658. This all changed when Lewis Carroll published *Alice's Adventures in Wonderland* with the express purpose of entertaining his young readers. To this day, we recognize that in order to teach children, we have to capture and retain their interest.

Alice's Adventures in Wonderland is a good book to use in a unit devoted to children's theater not only for the reasons stated above. Because it is "episodic," each individual chapter contains a complete story that can be easily adapted into a short play scene. The chapters can be taken out of order and some can even be skipped without disrupting the overall storyline.

Adapting a literary text is a great way to introduce children to an important work of literature. And the process of adaptation gives them a much deeper understanding of the text than they would get from reading alone. To be able to adapt a text, you must have a thorough understanding of the text.

There are a number of benefits of theater. As early as the fifth century BC, Aristotle recognized the cathartic effect of watching a play performed. More recently, Gardner's theory of multiple intelligences has shown that students learn in a variety of ways including visual, auditory, and kinesthetic. All of these modalities are addressed in theater. Kinesthetic learners probably will benefit the most in this project, but research suggests that we all learn better with some physical activity. An exercise break at the office. A walk during the lunch hour. The seventh inning stretch. I sometimes have students get up for a stretch to break up an hour-long lecture so they can wake up and shake out the cobwebs in their brains.

What other kinds of children might especially benefit from the theater unit?

▶ Creative

▶ Non-native speakers

▶ Extroverts . . . and introverts

Throughout this unit, alongside your instructions are suggestions for adapting these same instructions for your own students.

If you are like most of my students, you will probably find this to be the most fun unit in the book. Enjoy!

The Project

Create a dramatic adaptation of *Alice's Adventures in Wonderland*

Lesson One: Create the Groups

Lesson Two: Choose a Chapter

Lesson Three: Read the Book

Lesson Four: Brainstorm the Concept

Lesson Five: Pick a Part

Lesson Six: Write the Dialogue

Lesson Seven: Add the Action

Lesson Eight: Rehearse and Perform

Lesson Nine: Research and Reflect

Lesson Ten: Prepare to Teach

Lesson

©cs333/Shutterstock.com

Create the Groups

The first step:

What is often the worst thing about group work? That's right: the group! You can probably recall at least one bad experience of being in a group with members who did not get along with one another, or where one or more of the members would not participate equitably. With college-aged students, problems like this can usually be avoided by allowing them to choose their own group members. However, such an approach can cause several problems with younger students.

Therefore, your first step when you design your unit plan based on this project will have to be determining the best approach to creating the groups for your students.

The next step:

One approach that often works well with a large group of youngsters who don't know one another well is to use some form of a lottery. You could put their names in a hat and have them choose, according to groups, or, conversely, you could put the group numbers in a hat for them to pull out randomly.

Another method is to have them count out by the number of groups you wish to create. If you want to put twenty students into five groups of four each, you could simply have them call out the numbers one, two, three, four, five, as you go around the room, row by row. The downside to this approach is that your clever students may be working out the math in advance and, to avoid a group, may try to switch seats with a classmate.

The final step:

Assuming that your groups consist of students who may not know one another—or even if they do—a good way to promote camaraderie that is so important at this stage is to have some sort of structured ice breaker. You might ask them to start by just sharing their first names and then something easy, such as any pets they have, or their favorite television show. Your goal is to have them begin making connections among the other students and begin to feel a sense of "belonging" to their group. The more they feel connected, the less likely they will be to slack on their role within the group once the real work begins.

Lesson

©cs333/Shutterstock.com

Choose a Chapter

The first step:

Students of all ages, from elementary school to university, must have their chapters assigned to them. Left to their own devices, a university class of forty-five students will end up with six tea party scenes and four hookah-smoking caterpillars!

Therefore, some sort of lottery must be used. With the chapter numbers in the Mad Hatter's hat, each group can randomly select a number.

There are twleve chapters in the book; depending on the number of groups to be created, one or more chapters will need to be eliminated. Chapter 1 is essential in getting Alice into Wonderland. And Chapters 11 and 12 are essential in bringing Alice back to reality, they cannot be eliminated, or Alice will forever be lost in Wonderland.

Chapters that can most easily be eliminated without destroying the overall storyline are:

      3 <u>A Caucus-Race and a Long Tale</u>

      4 <u>The Rabbit Sends in a Little Bill</u>

      9 <u>The Mock Turtle's Story</u>

      10 <u>The Lobster Quadrille</u>

The next step:

Each group should begin by looking over their own chapter. Because *Alice's Adventures in Wonderland* is an "episodic" novel, it is perfectly acceptable to read a chapter out of context. Given the understanding that, after Chapter 1 and until Chapter 12, all of the chapters present a discreet episode with the introduction of unique characters. Alice is the only character to appear in each chapter, and one of the interesting aspects of this project is the variety of interpretations to this character that each group will present.

Alice is a diverse character, and in any given scene a different—sometimes contradictory—element of her personality may be expressed. She can be brave or frightened, polite or rude, but she is ever curious. The multiple times throughout the book that she changes size are a metaphorical representation of her feeling—like all children—at times quite grown-up and other times still very much a child.

The final step:

Now look at the other characters that are present in your chapter. Some of them—like the Cheshire Cat or the White Rabbit—appear in multiple scenes. But many others—like the Caterpillar or the Mad Hatter—do not.

Consider adding an entirely new character from our contemporary times or popular culture. Your new character can be an addition to the cast already in your chapter: Spongebob Squarepants unexpectedly crashes the tea party.

Or your new character can be a replacement for one of the original characters: Spongebob takes the place of the Mad Hatter.

Naturally, your new character should be one that children would recognize and find humorous. You don't want to invite Donald Trump or Eleanor Roosevelt to your tea party!

FEATURE

THE CHAPTERS

I	Down the Rabbit-Hole
II	The Pool of Tears
III	A Caucus-Race and a Long Tale
IV	The Rabbit Sends in a Little Bill
V	Advice from a Caterpillar
VI	Pig and Pepper
VII	A Mad Tea-Party
VIII	The Queen's Croquet-Ground
IX	The Mock Turtle's Story
X	The Lobster Quad
XI	Who Stole the Tarts?
XII	Alice's Evidence

**Be sure to read not only your chapter
but also the rest of the book!**

Lesson

©cs333/Shutterstock.com

Read the Book

The first step:

Don't forget to read not only your assigned chapter but also the rest of the book! To appreciate the creative work of each group, you will need to be familiar with the original version of their scene. The full text is available online in sites such as:

https://www.cs.cmu.edu/~rgs/alice-table.html

http://www.gutenberg.org/files/19033/19033-h/19033-h.htm

Alice in Wonderland was written by Lewis Carroll for a real girl named Alice Liddell. Carroll was a friend of Alice's family and would often make up stories to tell the three Liddell daughters. One summer day, after a riverside picnic, the girls begged him to tell them a story. He began by sending Alice down a rabbit hole, having no idea of what would happen to her next. Carroll made up Alice's adventures as he went along; several years later he wrote down the story from memory for publication.

Remember that this book, published in 1865, marked an important turning point in children's literature. Carroll's explicit goal was entertainment, not didacticism.

The next step:

In addition to reading the book, it is also very helpful to watch one or more film adaptations of the book. Many are readily available on YouTube or video outlets.

The first movie adaptation was the 1903 British silent film directed by Cecil Hepworth and Percy Stow. The film is interesting in its use of special effects, including Alice's shrinking in the Hall of Many Doors, and in her large size, stuck inside of White Rabbit's home, reaching through a window.

The most familiar is probably the 1951 animated musical produced by Walt Disney Productions. The film features the voices of Kathryn Beaumont as Alice, Sterling Holloway as the Cheshire Cat, Verna Felton as the Queen of Hearts, and Ed Wynn as the Mad Hatter. According to Wikipedia, "while the film was critically panned on its initial release, the movie proved to be ahead of its time and has since been regarded as one of Disney's greatest animated classics, notably one of the biggest cult classics in the animation medium, as well as one of the best film adaptations of *Alice*."

Two recent live-action adaptations include a television film first broadcast in 1999. Tina Majorino played the lead role of Alice, and a number of well-known performers portrayed the eccentric characters whom Alice meets during the course of the story, including Ben Kingsley, Ken Dodd, Martin Short, Whoopi Goldberg, Peter Ustinov, Christopher Lloyd, Gene Wilder, and Miranda Richardson.

And the film produced by Walt Disney Pictures and directed by Tim Burton, starring Johnny Depp as the Mad Hatter, Helena Bonham Carter as the Red Queen, Stephen Fry as the Cheshire Cat, and Mia Wasikowska as Alice that was released in 2010.

The final step:

After reading the book and viewing an adaptation or two, you might also find it helpful to consult one or more educational Web sites. In Scholastic's site, you'll find lesson plans to help to place the fantasy story within its dream-like context. One activity suggests that teachers remind their students that we enter a fantasy world when we dream or daydream. Students could create a "Dream Book" recording one of their dreams and create an illustration for the cover.

Another activity focuses on book covers and an analysis of the title itself. After distributing copies of *Alice in Wonderland,* the teacher could call students' attention to the cover illustration. They could then ask students "what clue they can find in the illustration that the book is a fantasy. . . . [and] why they think the place Alice visits is called Wonderland."

http://www.scholastic.com/teachers/lesson-plan/alice-wonderland-extension-activities

Lesson

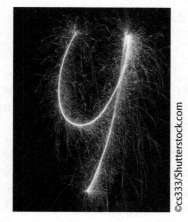

©cs333/Shutterstock.com

Brainstorm the Concept

The first step:

This is a creative project that begins by selecting material from the original text and then going off into creative directions. Begin by placing Alice into a modern setting. The time is now. The place is . . . where?

A hallmark of the genre of fantasy literature is the "scene of transformation": the moment when the main character journeys from the real and familiar world to another world that is surreal and unfamiliar.

In *Alice's Adventures in Wonderland*, the transition takes place as Alice falls down the rabbit hole. While falling, she notices familiar items: bookshelves, maps, pictures, and jars of orange marmalade. Familiar and also comforting items.

In *The Wonderful Wizard of Oz*, by L. Frank Baum, Dorothy is transported to Oz in the middle of a tornado, and her literally gray world turns bright and colorful. While she loses contact with her Aunt and Uncle, she does retain the familiar and comforting companion of her dog, Toto.

In *Harry Potter and the Sorcerer's Stone*, the original book of the Harry Potter series, by J.K. Rowling, Harry journeys to the wizardry world by train, via the magical Platform 9 ¾. On this fantastical train, he buys candies from the trolley, sharing them with his new friends and classmates.

The next step:

In your scene, you should create a similar melding of real and surreal elements, always remembering the comforting aspect of familiar items while navigating an unfamiliar terrain. When you went away to college, perhaps you packed a comforting item such as a Teddy bear or a favorite sweatshirt? So give your character, Alice, something that she can cling to in your scene.

The final step:

Writing is most often a solitary activity, but this kind of initial brainstorming is best done by bouncing ideas off of another person, or persons. Share with your group members. Listen to their ideas—respect-fully, of course. Let them inspire still more ideas of your own.

Collaboratively and collegially, come to an agreement among the members of your group regarding your concept. You should be able to articulate it in a sentence or two. For example: Alice falls down the rabbit hole and finds herself lost among the strange characters of modern-day New York City. Or: Alice is a freshman at the university and has to navigate the maze of unfamiliar buildings while encountering a range of idiosyncratic characters: friendly students and scary professors.

Now you have the framework upon which you can begin to build your scene.

FEATURE

©Morphart Creation/Shutterstock.com

Is Alice a good role model for children today?

It was all very well to say `Drink me,' but the wise little Alice was not going to do *that* in a hurry. `No, I'll look first,' she said, `and see whether it's marked "poison" or not'; for she had read several nice little histories about children who had got burnt, and eaten up by wild beasts and other unpleasant things, all because they *would* not remember the simple rules their friends had taught them: such as, that a red-hot poker will burn you if you hold it too long; and that if you cut your finger *very* deeply with a knife, it usually bleeds; and she had never forgotten that, if you drink much from a bottle marked 'poison,' it is almost certain to disagree with you, sooner or later. However, this bottle was *not* marked 'poison,' so Alice ventured to taste it, and finding it very nice, (it had, in fact, a sort of mixed flavor of cherry-tart, custard, pine-apple, roast turkey, toffee, and hot buttered toast) she very soon finished it off.

©Morphart Creation/Shutterstock.com

FEATURE

Analyzing Characters

Look at these illustrations by artist John Tenniel from the original 1865 edition of Alice's Adventures in Wonderland.

Based solely on the illustrations, and not what you know from reading the book, write a two- or three-sentence description of each character.

All images ©Morphart Creation/Shutterstock.com

Lesson

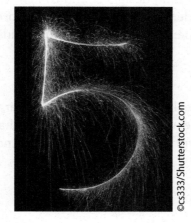

©cs333/Shutterstock.com

Pick a Part

The first step:

Make a list of characters that are in your book chapter.

There may be more characters than actors: what should you do? Actors can take on multiple parts, but should indicate their different roles with a distinctive piece of clothing such as a colorful hat or perhaps a sign around their neck. Or you can eliminate one or more of the characters.

There may be fewer characters than actors: what should you do? A narrator could be used to introduce the scene, played "in character" as someone participating in the scene or as an outside observer. Or you could add one or more original characters: an animal, a fantastic creature, Alice's sister, etc.

Each member in the group will need to play a part, and the casting of roles should be done democratically.

Start by casting Alice, the principle part. This role does not have to be open only to the female students in the group. Consider "gender-blind" casting, in which a male plays a female part. Or you could change the character's gender, in which it becomes "Alan's Adventures in Wonderland."

The next step:

In each group, every member must take on an equal share of the work. But in the theater, there are important parts to play behind the scenes as well. The more introverted members of the group may prefer to be in charge of stage or costume design, sound or light effects, or directing the scene. Being the director is a good role for shy students because it has them working very actively among the group members but not being thrust out to perform in front of the full audience.

The final step:

Don't forget the "role" of the audience. If your scene has more characters than actors, you could ask for a volunteer from the audience to come up on stage. Children love that! Just be sure that the part is small. Be sure to provide the lines clearly written on a sheet of paper. And never, ever, ask for a volunteer to take on an embarrassing role.

Lesson

Write the Dialogue

The first step:

This is the easy part: start by copying the lines of dialogue already in your scene.

For example, here's some of the dialogue between Alice and the Mouse in Chapter Two: The Pool of Tears:

> So she began, "O Mouse, do you know the way out of this pool? I am very tired of swimming about here, O Mouse!" The Mouse looked at her rather inquisitively and seemed to her to wink with one of its little eyes, but it said nothing.

> "Perhaps it doesn't understand English," thought Alice. "I dare say it's a French mouse, come over with William the Conqueror." So she began again: "Où est ma chatte?" which was the first sentence in her French lesson-book. The Mouse gave a sudden leap out of the water and seemed to quiver all over with fright. "Oh, I beg your pardon!" cried Alice hastily, afraid that she had hurt the poor animal's feelings. "I quite forgot you didn't like cats."

> "Not like cats!" cried the Mouse in a shrill, passionate voice. "Would you like cats, if you were me?"

Copy and paste only the spoken words, eliminating (for now) any prose narration. Put the speaker's name in all capital letters, followed by a colon—and no quotation marks. Double-space the lines between speakers, but single-space each individual speech. It should look like this:

> ALICE: O Mouse, do you know the way out of this pool? I am very tired of swimming about here. O Mouse! Perhaps it doesn't understand English. I dare say it's a French mouse, come over with William the Conqueror. Où est ma chatte? Oh, I beg your pardon! I quite forgot you didn't like cats.

> MOUSE: Not like cats! Would *you* like cats, if you were me?

The next step:

Modernize the text you copied, updating archaic words or phrases. Look over the speech you just copied. What words would you change and why?

Below are some words highlighted in bold that might sound strange to a modern child's ears. How would you modernize them?

> ALICE: O Mouse, do you know the way out of this pool? I am very tired of swimming **about** here. O Mouse! **Perhaps** it doesn't understand English. **I dare say** it's a French mouse, come over with William the Conqueror. Où est ma chatte? Oh, I beg your pardon! I **quite** forgot you didn't like cats.

> MOUSE: Not like cats! Would *you* like cats, if you were me?

Consider also the highlighted references below that might confuse a modern American child, not as familiar with European history or foreign languages. How might you change them to better relate to your students?

> ALICE: O Mouse, do you know the way out of this pool? I am very tired of swimming about here. O Mouse! Perhaps it doesn't understand English. I dare say **it's a French mouse, come over with William the Conqueror. Où est ma chatte?** Oh, I beg your pardon! I quite forgot you didn't like cats.

> MOUSE: Not like cats! Would *you* like cats, if you were me?

The final step:

Now you may add some stage directions, but only if they are essential for the actor playing the part. Don't tell them how to speak.

> MOUSE (in a shrill, passionate voice): Not like cats! Would *you* like cats, if you were me?

But do tell them what to do:

> MOUSE (running away): Not like cats! Would *you* like cats, if you were me?

Now comes the hardest part. Add your own original material and coordinate it with your group. Your goal is a cohesive and coherent ten-minute scene.

FEATURE

Choose one of the excerpts below and adapt the text, following the steps outlined in the previous Lesson.

©Morphart Creation/Shutterstock.com

CHAPTER 3

'But who has won?'

This question the Dodo could not answer without a great deal of thought, and it sat for a long time with one finger pressed upon its forehead (the position in which you usually see Shakespeare, in the pictures of him), while the rest waited in silence. At last the Dodo said, '*Everybody* has won, and all must have prizes.'

'But who is to give the prizes?' quite a chorus of voices asked.

'Why, *she*, of course,' said the Dodo, pointing to Alice with one finger; and the whole party at once crowded round her, calling out in a confused way, 'Prizes! Prizes!'

Alice had no idea what to do, and in despair she put her hand in her pocket, and pulled out a box of comfits, (luckily the salt water had not got into it), and handed them round as prizes. There was exactly one a-piece all round.

'But she must have a prize herself, you know,' said the Mouse.

'Of course,' the Dodo replied very gravely. 'What else have you got in your pocket?' he went on, turning to Alice.

'Only a thimble,' said Alice sadly.

'Hand it over here,' said the Dodo.

Then they all crowded round her once more, while the Dodo solemnly presented the thimble, saying 'We beg your acceptance of this elegant thimble.'

©Morphart Creation/Shutterstock.com

CHAPTER 7

'Why is a raven like a writing-desk?'

'Come, we shall have some fun now!' thought Alice. 'I'm glad they've begun asking riddles.—I believe I can guess that,' she added aloud.

'Do you mean that you think you can find out the answer to it?' said the March Hare.

'Exactly so,' said Alice.

'Then you should say what you mean,' the March Hare went on.

'I do,' Alice hastily replied; 'at least—at least I mean what I say—that's the same thing, you know.'

'Not the same thing a bit!' said the Hatter. 'You might just as well say that "I see what I eat" is the same thing as "I eat what I see"!'

'You might just as well say,' added the March Hare, 'that "I like what I get" is the same thing as "I get what I like"!'

©Morphart Creation/Shutterstock.com

CHAPTER 5

'Who are *you*?' said the Caterpillar.

This was not an encouraging opening for a conversation. Alice replied, rather shyly, 'I—I hardly know, sir, just at present—at least I know who I *was* when I got up this morning, but I think I must have been changed several times since then.'

'What do you mean by that?' said the Caterpillar sternly. 'Explain yourself!'

'I can't explain *myself*, I'm afraid, sir' said Alice, 'because I'm not myself, you see.'

'I don't see,' said the Caterpillar.

'I'm afraid I can't put it more clearly,' Alice replied very politely, 'for I can't understand it myself to begin with; and being so many different sizes in a day is very confusing.'

'It isn't,' said the Caterpillar.

All images ©Morphart Creation/Shutterstock.com

CHAPTER 9

'Look out now, Five! Don't go splashing paint over me like that!'

'I couldn't help it,' said Five, in a sulky tone; 'Seven jogged my elbow.'

On which Seven looked up and said, 'That's right, Five! Always lay the blame on others!'

'*You'd* better not talk!' said Five. 'I heard the Queen say only yesterday you deserved to be beheaded!'

'What for?' said the one who had spoken first.

'That's none of *your* business, Two!' said Seven.

'Yes, it *is* his business!' said Five, 'and I'll tell him—it was for bringing the cook tulip-roots instead of onions.'

Seven flung down his brush, and had just begun 'Well, of all the unjust things—' when his eye chanced to fall upon Alice, as she stood watching them, and he checked himself suddenly: the others looked round also, and all of them bowed low.

'Would you tell me,' said Alice, a little timidly, 'why you are painting those roses?'

©Morphart Creation/Shutterstock.com

CHAPTER 8

'Can you play croquet?'

The soldiers were silent, and looked at Alice, as the question was evidently meant for her.

'Yes!' shouted Alice.

'Come on, then!' roared the Queen, and Alice joined the procession, wondering very much what would happen next.

'It's—it's a very fine day!' said a timid voice at her side. She was walking by the White Rabbit, who was peeping anxiously into her face.

'Very,' said Alice: '—where's the Duchess?'

'Hush! Hush!' said the Rabbit in a low, hurried tone. He looked anxiously over his shoulder as he spoke, and then raised himself upon tiptoe, put his mouth close to her ear, and whispered 'She's under sentence of execution.'

'What for?' said Alice.

'Did you say "What a pity!"?' the Rabbit asked.

'No, I didn't,' said Alice: 'I don't think it's at all a pity. I said "What for?"'

'She boxed the Queen's ears—' the Rabbit began. Alice gave a little scream of laughter. 'Oh, hush!' the Rabbit whispered in a frightened tone. 'The Queen will hear you! You see, she came rather late, and the Queen said—'

'Get to your places!' shouted the Queen in a voice of thunder.

Children will not sit still for a "talky" play.

Involve your audience!

Lesson

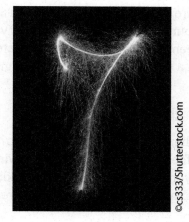

©cs333/Shutterstock.com

Add the Action

The first step:

Children will not sit still for a "talky" scene. You must move or they will, fidgeting in their seats. The sillier your actions, the more your children will delight in them. You just have to leave your serious adult behavior in the wings when you enter the stage, and run, skip, hop, or boogie to your best beat.

But what if your scene doesn't contain any such actions in the book chapter your group is adapting? And what if you can't see a justifiable reason for Alice to jump up and down as she is growing or shrinking, or for the Cheshire Cat to suddenly break into a bit of break dancing?

Congratulations: you have created a "suddenly."

The next step:

In *Theater for Children: A Guide to Writing, Adapting, Directing, and Acting* (1999), David Wood and Janet Grant discuss the use of "suddenlies"—unexpected actions or plot twists. A character shows up when least expected. A bizarre prop emerges, perhaps one that defies the normal "scale" of things: an enormous mouse beside a tiny elephant. After all, we are in Wonderland, where anything is possible.

"Above all, keep the action flowing. Find enough suddenlies. . . ." (Wood and Grant 73).

The final step:

Involve the audience. Earlier, you were asked to consider involving an individual member of the audience as a volunteer to take on an extra role.

Now consider ways to involve the entire audience. What might you ask them to do in your scene? Before you start tossing around ideas with your group partners, have everyone take a minute to write out a list of possible ideas—no matter how seemingly lame or inappropriate. The goal is to create the longest possible list. You might even make it a competition to see which group member can come up with the longest list.

Some ways to involve the audience might be:

▶ respond to a question ("Where did the White Rabbit go?"—this kind of question appeals to children as it gives them a feeling of superiority in knowing something that the actors, apparently, don't know. "Can anyone find his gloves?"—this kind of question can get the students up out of their chairs and exploring the theater, but be ready to rein the chaos when it's time to return to the play)

▶ join in a physical activity with the actors on stage (playing croquet or dancing the lobster quadrille or serving as members of the jury)

▶ make sound effects with their voice ("shhhh-shhhh" for the sound of the waves in the Pool of Tears") or clapping their hands or stamping their feet.

What else did you and your group come up with?

FEATURE

Some actions might seem impossible to stage. Look at each of the actions represented below and come up with a clever way that they could be staged.

All images ©Morphart Creation/Shutterstock.com

Lesson

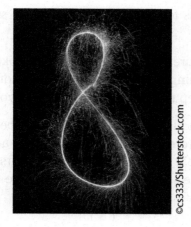

©cs333/Shutterstock.com

Rehearse . . . and Perform!

The first step....

Get up on your feet!!!

For some reason, many adult students find this to be the hardest step, while it comes so naturally to younger students.

Much of this unit has been completed while seated and reading, brainstorming, writing, but without ample time for on-your-feet rehearsal, you will find yourself stumbling over your fellow actors when it's time for the show to go on.

Now is the time to work out the appropriate "blocking": that is, entrances and exits for each character, optimum placement on the stage so that each actor can be seen and heard.

This can all be in the hands of a designated director, or worked out democratically with suggestions from each member of the group. Often it is difficult to direct yourself, so be sure to remain open to helpful suggestions from your fellow actors.

The next step:

As you do a full, non-stop run-through of the scene, set your stopwatch to check the timing. This, too, is best done on your feet, as the movements and actions will affect the overall running time of your scene.

Remember that your assignment calls for a ten-minute scene. Be sure that your material does not fall short of the time.

Your rehearsal work should also ensure a smooth set-up and "strike" of your scene. You do not want your audience to get impatient watching you setting up your backdrop or props; nor do you want to go over your allotted time frame and keep the next group waiting as you take your props down.

The "dress" rehearsal is the time to add visual elements to your scene: colorful costumes, fun props, or backdrops will help to capture the interest of the children in your audience. Special effects can include the use of lights and/or sounds. Simply turning the classroom lights on or off can help to set the mood, or signal the beginning and end of the scene. Consider appropriate "pre-show" music that you can play as your group sets up.

The final step:

The show must go on!

On performance day, it's important to remind your students that the audience plays the most important role of all. They must be attentive and appropriately responsive, but always respectful and quiet when necessary.

As a closing activity, you should engage in a "review" of each scene. Naturally, you will want to focus on the positive. Consider such questions as:

- ▶ Which scene had the most unusual audience involvement?

- ▶ Which "suddenly" was the most surprising?

- ▶ How would you compare the different Alices from each scene and what different aspects of her personality were brought to life?

Lesson

©cs333/Shutterstock.com

Research and Reflect

The first step:

A good teacher is always reflecting on the classroom experience, through both informal and formal assessment.

- ► What worked well?

- ► What surprised you?

- ► What would you do differently?

- ► What do you think your students learned?

- ► Did your students learn what you had intended; in other words, did you meet your objective?

Therefore, each of our four units will involve a short written reflection as a summative experience.

The next step:

After completing the children's theater project, compose a thesis-driven 1,000-word essay incorporating outside research with your own reflection on the experience.

The bibliography listed at the end of this book contains a number of reliable outside sources, or you may prefer to consult the library or check additional online Web sites.

You may, if you wish, include quotations from *Alice's Adventures in Wonderland*, but these are "primary texts" and do not count as "research" material.

The standard five-paragraph theme format is useful for such a short paper:

- ► State your thesis

- ► Support it with a brief quotation from one or two outside sources

- ► Briefly describe what you did in the theater project....

- ► . . . and what you learned

- ► Restate your thesis indicating that it is supported by your research and firsthand experience

Yes, it is permissible—even desirable—in a reflection essay to use the first person ("I").

Keep in mind that a thesis is not just a topic sentence: "This essay is about children's theater." It contains both the topic and an opinion: "Children's theater is an effective way to address kinesthetic learners."

For this project, a possible thesis might be: "Adapting a familiar story such as *Alice's Adventures in Wonderland* can be used to present a lesson about respecting seemingly odd characters." It could be supported by a scene in which Alice makes a new friend.

The final step:

After drafting your essay, be sure that you have included proper citations for any quoted or paraphrased materials, following MLA citation format. The Purdue University Web site is a helpful resource for MLA format questions:

https://owl.english.purdue.edu/owl/resource/747/01/

Finally, proofread carefully for spelling, grammar, or punctuation errors.

Lesson

©cs333/Shutterstock.com

Prepare to Teach

The first step:

In the project that you completed for this unit, you worked with a group of your classmates to present just one short scene. When you begin teaching, you will need to expand this project into a full week-long unit plan—resulting in a full-length adaptation of the entire book.

Your unit plan should open with a context statement or rationale for the unit. Before describing what you will do each day, step back and think about WHY you are presenting a unit like this. Why do you think it is valuable for your students to spend a week creating an original adaptation of a work of literature for the stage? And, in particular, why is it beneficial for them to be working with their classmates on this group project?

Assume that you will devote one class hour to the lesson on each day. Then design the specific activities, along with your objectives or goals for what you hope your students will learn each day.

Be careful not to confuse "objective" with "activity."

"Watch a film version of *Alice's Adventures in Wonderland*."—This is an activity, something you will *do* with your students in this lesson.

"Understand how the film incorporates elements from the book while adding original creative elements."—This is an objective, something you want your students to *learn* through the lesson.

The next step:

Design a daily lesson plan template that works for you. You can get ideas from Web sites or education manuals, but ultimately it is a matter of individual preference. Some essential categories to include are:

- objectives

- materials needed

- activities

- assessments

But whether you list them in this order or a different order, whether you put the information in boxes or columns, and whether the information is expressed in complete sentences or fragments in a bulleted list: all of this is up to your personal discretion.

A sample lesson plan is provided on the following page.

The final step . . .

Connect to core standards, as applicable in your state. You should consult the Department of Education Web site for current standards for your state. For example:

http://www.doe.in.gov/standards/englishlanguage-arts

Evaluation Sheet

NAME _____

This sheet MUST be submitted during your presentation!

	Poor	**Satisfactory**	**Outstanding**

OVERALL:

Active participation in group

Equitable role within group

THE BOOK:

Creative and original

Connection to the text

NO misspelled words

PRESENTATION:

Prepared and polished

GRADE: _____

Unit Four

Adolescent Fiction

(Grades 7–8)

"TOM!"

No answer.

"TOM!"

No answer.

"What's gone with that boy, I wonder? You TOM!"

No answer.

The old lady pulled her spectacles down and looked over them about the room; then she put them up and looked out under them. She seldom or never looked *through* them for so small a thing as a boy; they were her state pair, the pride of her heart, and were built for "style," not service—she could have seen through a pair of stove-lids just as well. She looked perplexed for a moment, and then said, not fiercely, but still loud enough for the furniture to hear:

"Well, I lay if I get hold of you I'll—"

She did not finish, for by this time she was bending down and punching under the bed with the broom, and so she needed breath to punctuate the punches with. She resurrected nothing but the cat.

"I never did see the beat of that boy!"

—*The Adventures of Tom Sawyer*, Mark Twain (1884)

In this unit, we'll revisit a classic example of adolescent fiction that you probably read as an adolescent yourself. It is a great story of nineteenth century Middle America, as seen through the unique experiences of an adolescent boy. In addition to entertaining the reader with Tom's many adventures, and misadventures, the novel also addresses serious issues of racial relations and slavery.

According to the NEH Web site for teachers:

Great stories articulate and explore the mysteries of our daily lives in the larger context of the human struggle. The writer's voice, style, and use of language inform the plot, characters, and themes. By creating opportunities to learn, imagine, and reflect, a great novel is a work of art that affects many generations of readers, changes lives, challenges assumptions, and breaks new ground.

—http://neabigread.org/teachers_guides/lesson_plans/adventuresoftomsawyer

In this unit, while exploring this and other examples of adolescent fiction, including a number of Newbery Award winning books, we will also connect this genre of literature for older students with an important issue: juvenile delinquency. Tom Sawyer skips school, bullies the new kid, and runs away from home. Is that innocent boyish behavior, or is it a precursor to more serious delinquency?

Compare this novel to a contemporary novel, *The Watsons Go to Birmingham 1963*, by Christopher Paul Curtis. Like Twain's novel, this too combines boyish adventures with historical issues, in this case, race relations in the 1960s. The novel's narrator, ten-year-old Kenny, calls his thirteen-year-old brother Byron "an official juvenile delinquent." Byron is a bully who skips school, plays with fire, and beats up on younger kids. Is that delinquency?

Very likely the authors of both of these books would say no, but their charming examples of boyhood mischief do provide a good opportunity to raise this issue with your adolescent students.

At what stage does "innocent" mischief become "serious" trouble? And what can be done to prevent an adolescent from crossing that line?

These questions—along with what makes good literature—will be explored in this unit.

The Project

Read one Newbery Award novel that connects to our theme of juvenile delinquency.

Use your chosen novel to teach your students about literature and also about this important issue.

Lesson One: Consult the Newberys

Lesson Two: Choose a Book

Lesson Three: Analyze the Book

Lesson Four: Characters and Setting

Lesson Five: Plot and Themes

Lesson Six: Language

Lesson Seven: Present Your Book

Lesson Eight: Discuss Juvenile Delinquency

Lesson Nine: Research and Reflect

Lesson Ten: Prepare to Teach

Lesson

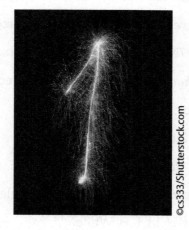

©cs333/Shutterstock.com

Consult the Newberys

The first step:

As you did in the Picture Book unit, you need to start by looking at some of the best books ever published in this genre. The gold standard for adolescent fiction is the annual Newbery Award, established in 1922.

You can access information about the award and a comprehensive list of annual winners through the American Library Association Web site:

http://www.ala.org/alsc/awardsgrants/bookmedia/newberymedal/newberyhonors/newberymedal

Some notable books from recent years include:

2004 Medal Winner: *The Tale of Despereaux: Being the Story of a Mouse, a Princess, Some Soup, and a Spool of Thread* by Kate DiCamillo

2000 Medal Winner: *Bud, Not Buddy* by Christopher Paul Curtis

1999 Medal Winner: *Holes* by Louis Sachar

1997 Medal Winner: *The View from Saturday* by E.L. Konigsburg

1996 Honor Book: *The Watsons Go to Birmingham: 1963* by Christopher Paul Curtis

1994 Medal Winner: The *Giver* by Lois Lowry

1990 Medal Winner: *Number the Stars* by Lois Lowry

1986 Medal Winner: *Sarah, Plain and Tall* by Patricia MacLachlan

1981 Medal Winner: *Jacob Have I Loved* by Katherine Paterson

1978 Medal Winner: *Bridge to Terabithia* by Katherine Paterson

1977 Medal Winner: *Roll of Thunder, Hear My Cry* by Mildred D. Taylor

1970 Medal Winner: *Sounder* by William H. Armstrong

Some "classics" from earlier years include:

1968 Medal Winner: *From the Mixed-Up Files of Mrs. Basil E. Frankweiler* by E.L. Konigsburg

1963 Medal Winner: *A Wrinkle in Time* by Madeleine L'Engle

1953 Honor Book: *Charlotte's Web* by E.B. White

1944 Medal Winner: *Johnny Tremain* by Esther Forbes

1934 Medal Winner: *Invincible Louisa: The Story of the Author of Little Women* by Cornelia Meigs

1933 Honor Book: *The Railroad To Freedom: A Story of the Civil War* by Hildegarde Swift

1923 Medal Winner: *The Voyages of Doctor Dolittle* by Hugh Lofting

Examining books such as these will give you a good idea of what qualities make a successful novel for young readers.

The next step:

Research some of the books online, through sites such as Amazon.com. Through online sources, you can find more information about the books and even useful teaching tools for educators.

As you did with the picture books, ask yourself questions such as:

THE TITLE

Is it compelling and evocative, or confusing and unclear?

Based on the title alone, what do you expect the book to be about?

THE COVER

Are the graphics impressionistic cartoons, realistic drawings, or photographs?

Is the tone serious or humorous?

The final step:

Locate one or more of the books in the library so that you can read them in full. It's unlikely, but if you are unable to locate any Newbery books, browse the library's holdings for other books that connect with our theme of juvenile delinquency.

Lesson

©cs333/Shutterstock.com

Choose a Book

The first step:

Choosing a book you've already read, as an adult or a young reader, has both advantages and disadvantages. If you read it as an adolescent yourself, you are in a good position to understand a young reader's perspective on the novel. But by choosing a book you already know, you are cheating yourself of the opportunity to expand your knowledge of additional books.

Instead, consider asking adolescents you know what their favorite books are. Or ask teachers of middle school to recommend books that they have found to be popular among their students or that connect appropriately with the theme of our unit.

The next step:

Now that you have some titles from teachers, students, and/or the Newbery list, go ahead and take a look at some unfamiliar books. Make a list of the books. Start with the titles that intrigue you most. Then consider the characters; do you want a "boy book" or a "girl book"? That may sound sexist, but it simply refers to the protagonist. Is the hero of the story male or female?

Do you prefer first-person narrators, in which the protagonist tells his or her own story, often addressing the reader directly? These kinds of novels are usually more entertaining and quicker to read.

Perhaps it's the setting that will attract you to one book over another. Do you enjoy books that have urban settings, or rural settings? American or foreign? Set in the present day or future or back in an historical period?

Finally, do you want a book that is contemporary, published within recent years, or one of the earlier Newbery winners, perhaps during a significant era such as the 1940s or 1960s?

The final step:

Newbery award-winning books are a good and guaranteed source of high-quality literature, recognized by the Newbery judges to be deserving of study.

Other good sources of adolescent fiction that connect to the theme of juvenile delinquency are books such as:

> *Bookfinder: A Guide to Children's Literature about the Needs & Problems of Youth Aged 2 to 15* by Sharon S. Dreyer (1989)

> *Adolescents At Risk: A Guide to Fiction and Nonfiction for Young Adults, Parents, and Professionals* by Joan Kaywell (1993)

Kaywell includes chapters on alienation and identity, drugs and alcohol, stress and suicide.

Among the fiction titles in her extensive bibliography are:

> *Are you there, God? It's Me, Margaret*

> *The Goats*

> *Brian's Song*

> *Bridge to Terabithia*

> *The Other Side of the Mountain*

> *Sarah, Plain and Tall*

> *The Outsiders*

> *Catcher in the Rye*

Also included are nonfiction titles, such as *Portrait of a Teenage Alcoholic* and *How to Keep It Together When Your Parents are Coming Apart.*

FEATURE

Compare the following short editorial descriptions of four books on Amazon.com.

Which of the following books sounds most appropriate for a unit dealing with juvenile delinquency?

1. Sara Louise Bradshaw is sick and tired of her beautiful twin Caroline. Ever since they were born, Caroline has been the pretty one, the talented one, the better sister. Even now, Caroline seems to take everything: Louise's friends, their parents' love, her dreams for the future.

For once in her life, Louise wants to be the special one. But in order to do that, she must first figure out who she is and find a way to make a place for herself outside her sister's shadow.

—*Jacob Have I Loved,* by Katherine Paterson

2. This winner of the Newbery Medal and the National Book Award features Stanley Yelnats, a kid who is under a curse. A curse that began with his no-good-dirty-rotten-pig-stealing-great-great-grandfather and has since followed generations of Yelnats. Now Stanley has been unjustly sent to a boys' detention center, Camp Green Lake, where the warden makes the boys "build character" by spending all day, every day, digging holes five feet wide and five feet deep. It doesn't take long for Stanley to realize there's more than character improvement going on at Camp Green Lake: the warden is looking for something. Stanley tries to dig up the truth in this inventive and darkly humorous tale of crime and punishment—and redemption.

—*Holes,* by Louis Sachar

3. A wonderful middle-grade novel narrated by Kenny, nine, about his middle-class black family, the Weird Watsons of Flint, Michigan. When Kenny's thirteen-year-old brother, Byron, gets to be too much trouble, they head south to Birmingham to visit Grandma, the one person who can shape him up. And they happen to be in Birmingham when Grandma's church is blown up.

—*The Watsons Go to Birmingham 1963,* by Christopher Paul Curtis

4. When suburban Claudia Kincaid decides to run away, she knows she doesn't just want to run *from* somewhere she wants to run *to* somewhere—to a place that is comfortable, beautiful, and preferably elegant. She chooses the Metropolitan Museum of Art in New York City. Knowing that her younger brother, Jamie, has money and thus can help her with the serious cash flow problem she invites him along. Once settled into the museum, Claudia and Jamie find themselves caught up in the mystery of an angel statue that the museum purchased at an auction for a bargain price of $250. The statue is possibly an early work of the Renaissance master Michelangelo, and therefore worth millions. Is it? Or isn't it? Claudia is determined to find out. This quest leads Claudia to Mrs. Basil E. Frankweiler, the remarkable old woman who sold the statue and to some equally remarkable discoveries about herself.

—*From the Mixed-Up Files of Mrs. Basil E. Frankweiler,* by E.L. Konigsburg

Five Literary Elements

1   Plot

2. Character

3. Setting

4. Theme

5. Language

Lesson

©cs333/Shutterstock.com

Analyze the Book

The first step:

When you introduce your students to a work of literature, you will find it useful to begin with the five essential literary elements. That may sound daunting at first, but when you tell a friend about a movie, you probably take the same approach. What movie have you seen recently? Write down three sentences in which you tell a friend about it.

Now look at what you wrote. You probably started with character (who is in it), perhaps followed by setting (where/when does the story take place).

Here's one way to describe *The Martian*:

> During a mission to Mars, Astronaut Mark Watney is presumed dead and left behind by his crew. But Watney has survived and finds himself stranded on the hostile planet. With only meager supplies, he must find a way to signal to Earth that he is alive.
>
> —http://www.imdb.com/title/tt3659388/

Start with character: *Astronaut Mark Watney*. Then describe the setting: *Mars . . . the hostile planet*.

The next step:

Almost certainly, it was only after you mentioned the main character[s] and setting did you get to the plot (what happens). You may also have touched on themes (what issues the movie deals with; this is slightly different from simply stating what happens).

Briefly summarize the main plot: *Watney is presumed dead and left behind by his crew . . . he must find a way to signal to Earth that he is alive.*

Identify one or more themes: *survival against impossible odds.*

The final step:

The fifth literary element is language (did the main character tell his own story, or was there a narrator?).

In a work of literature, language entails several elements. Does the book have a first-person or third-person narrator? How would you describe the narrator's "voice": formal or informal? Childlike or grown-up?

Andy Weir's sci-fi novel *The Martian* (2014), which was adapted into the 2016 movie, opens with a "log entry" that states:

> Six days into what should be the greatest two months of my life, and it's turned into a nightmare.
>
> I don't even know who'll read this. I guess someone will find it eventually. Maybe a hundred years from now.
>
> ….
>
> Let's see…where do I begin?

Compare that very informal first-person language to the third-person omniscient narrator in the opening of *Tom Sawyer*.

Lesson

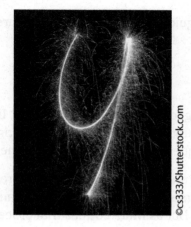

©cs333/Shutterstock.com

Characters and Setting

The first step:

Make a list of the main characters in Tom Sawyer, with two or three words to describe each. Tom is obviously the central character, also known as the hero or the "protagonist." A good writer will create multi-dimensional characters, having both positive and negative qualities. What are Tom's negative qualities, or flaws?

The NEA Big Read Web site suggests that a protagonist usually initiates the main action of the story and often overcomes a flaw, such as weakness or ignorance, to achieve a "new understanding" by the work's end. Aristotle considered these to be "tragic flaws," which can lead to the protagonist's downfall.

A protagonist who acts with honor or courage is called a hero. In this novel, Tom clearly serves as the protagonist. Do you consider him a hero? Why, or why not?

An antihero is a protagonist lacking in heroic qualities. Instead of being "dignified, brave, idealistic, or purposeful," the antihero may be "cowardly, self-interested, or weak." Is there an antihero in this novel? If so, who is it?

Other characters may serve as "foils" with traits that contrast with the protagonist's and highlight features of the main character's personality. These serve to offset one or more of the protagonist's characteristics or behaviors. Who do you see as foils to Tom? Obvious foils are Huck and Sid, but what about Aunt Polly and Becky?

—http://neabigread.org/teachers_guides/lesson_plans/adventuresoftomsawyer/Twain_TG2014.pdf

The next step:

How have the main characters changed by the end of the book? In most novels, the development of characters occurs through their encounters with a series of challenges. These may be internal or external forces that require characters to question themselves, overcome fears, or reconsider dreams.

Consider the process of Tom's maturation throughout the novel, reflecting his character development. In Chapter Ten, after witnessing the murder of Dr. Robinson, he and Huck take a blood oath that they will never tell anyone what they saw. But as Muff Potter's trial proceeds toward the certainty of a guilty verdict, Tom suffers increasing torments of conscience, leading to a very mature decision.

The final step:

The setting is extremely important in understanding a book like Tom Sawyer. Setting refers not only to where (Missouri) but also when (nineteenth century). Why is that setting significant?

What kind of scenes take place indoors versus outdoors?

Compare the tone of the following pairs of indoor/outdoor scenes:

> Chapter Four in Sunday school vs. Chapter Nine in the graveyard
>
> Chapter Thirteen on the raft vs. Chapter Thirty-Four in the Widow Douglas's home.

In general, the outdoors tends to be a liberating environment; the indoors, more restrictive even stifling.

Lesson

Plot and Themes

The first step:

Plot is simply what happens. The plot of any novel (or film) can be expressed through verbs, "action words." What did the character do? What happened to him or her?

In one or two sentences, sum up the basic plot of Tom Sawyer. Then, consider any sub-plots that run parallel to the main plot, perhaps shedding a different light on the main plot itself.

The plot doesn't have to unravel in chronological order. Foreshadowing and flashbacks are often employed in novels to create a unique twist or turn of events. The peak of the story's conflict is the "climax," which is followed by the story's resolution, or "denouement."

The next step:

Of the five essential literary elements, theme may be the most important, and for many students, it may be the most difficult to identify. It is easy to identify the main character and to summarize what happens to him. It is harder to identify the main theme because most works of literature have more than one theme. There is also a certain degree of subjectivity involved. Three different readers reading the same book may well identify three different themes as being the so-called main one.

Themes are simply the issues that are addressed in a novel. Classic themes in adolescent fiction are family relations, adolescent love, or growing up. A novel often reconsiders these perennial issues by presenting them in new contexts or from new points of view. All works of literature contain more than one theme. What are some themes in *Tom Sawyer*?

The final step:

While there are multiple themes in any work of literature, in this unit, we will focus on the theme of juvenile delinquency. Where in the book do you find examples of this theme?

Be aware, however, that looking at a work of literature from just one lens may provide a distorted vision of the overall work. While we may focus on the issue of juvenile delinquency for the purpose of this unit, we don't want to come away with the idea that *Tom Sawyer* is a novel about juvenile delinquency. It is a novel about so much more than can be expressed in any one theme.

Lesson

©cs333/Shutterstock.com

Language

The first step:

"TOM!"

No answer.

"TOM!"

No answer.

"What's gone with that boy, I wonder? You TOM!"

No answer.

The old lady pulled her spectacles down and looked over them about the room....

The next step:

Two other elements of language are dialogue and dialect. Be sure not to confuse these two terms.

DIALOGUE is two, or more, people in conversation:

> "There! I might 'a' thought of that closet. What you been doing in there?"

> "Nothing."

> "Nothing! Look at your hands. And look at your mouth. What IS that truck?"

> "I don't know, aunt."

> "Well, I know. It's jam—that's what it is. Forty times I've said if you didn't let that jam alone I'd skin you. Hand me that switch."

The final step:

DIALECT is the unique way of speaking of some characters, such as Aunt Polly:

> Hang the boy, can't I never learn anything? Ain't he played me tricks enough like that for me to be looking out for him by this time? But old fools is the biggest fools there is. Can't learn an old dog new tricks, as the saying is. But my goodness, he never plays them alike, two days, and how is a body to know what's coming? He 'pears to know just how long he can torment me before I get my dander up, and he knows if he can make out to put me off for a minute or make me laugh, it's all down again and I can't hit him a lick. I ain't doing my duty by that boy, and that's the Lord's truth, goodness knows.

Or the slave Jim:

> Can't, Mars Tom. Ole missis, she tole me I got to go an' git dis water an' not stop foolin' roun' wid anybody. She say she spec' Mars Tom gwine to ax me to whitewash, an' so she tole me go 'long an' 'tend to my own business—she 'lowed SHE'D 'tend to de whitewash-in'. . . . Ole missis she'd take an' tar de head off'n me. 'Deed she would.

Lesson

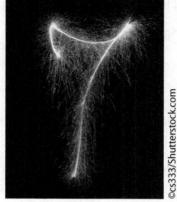

©cs333/Shutterstock.com

Present Your Book

The first step:

Now that you have chosen an appropriate book and analyzed it in terms of the five essential literary elements, you are ready to present your book to your students. When you create the week-long unit plan, you will be delving into the entire book in detail. For this assignment, you are introducing the book in your first lesson.

Create a PowerPoint or Prezi presentation of ten slides. If possible, select a template that somehow matches the tone, theme, or setting of your book, For example, a nautical backdrop if the book deals with the sea.

Each slide should contain engaging and appropriate graphics. Try to make use of attention-grabbing transitions and animations on each slide. Be sure that the font is legible and not obscured by background colors.

The first slide should give the title of the book, its author, and publication date. The graphic could be a reproduction of the book cover.

The next step:

In the next eight slides, present the five essential elements. How you divide those slides will depend on your book and the way in which you choose to present it. You might want to use a separate slide for four main characters, leaving slides six through nine for the remaining four literary elements. Or, if the book has two separate settings, perhaps you'll want to use two slides for the settings.

The tenth slide should contain an intriguing question to get your students interested in—ideally, even excited about—reading the book.

The final step:

You could consider incorporating music or a short video clip from a film adaptation of your book, if there is one.

It's always a good idea to practice a presentation out loud, checking your time and ensuring that you don't stumble over the pronunciation of any awkward phrases or unfamiliar names.

Finally, be sure to proofread carefully: every slide MUST be entirely free of any errors in spelling, grammar, or punctuation.

FEATURE

READ THE PASSAGE BELOW AND CONSIDER WHETHER THESE BOYS ARE ENGAGED IN APPROPRIATE ADOLESCENT BEHAVIOR, OR EXHIBITING SIGNS OF FUTURE TROUBLE.

Neither boy spoke. If one moved, the other moved—but only side-wise, in a circle; they kept face to face and eye to eye all the time. Finally Tom said:

"I can lick you!"

"I'd like to see you try it."

"Well, I can do it."

"No you can't, either."

"Yes I can."

"No you can't."

"I can."

"You can't."

"Can!"

"Can't!"

An uncomfortable pause. Then Tom said:

"What's your name?"

"'Tisn't any of your business, maybe."

"Well I 'low I'll MAKE it my business."

"Well why don't you?"

"If you say much, I will."

"Much—much—MUCH. There now.". . .

"Aw—take a walk!"

"Say—if you give me much more of your sass I'll take and bounce a rock off'n your head."

"Oh, of COURSE you will."

"Well I WILL."

"Well why don't you DO it then? What do you keep SAYING you will for? Why don't you DO it? It's because you're afraid."

"I AIN'T afraid."

"You are."

"I ain't."

"You are."

Another pause, and more eying and sidling around each other. Presently they were shoulder to shoulder.

Why do you think Tom Sawyer bullies the new kid?

What is he after in this chapter?

Lesson

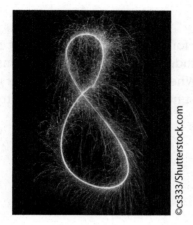

©cs333/Shutterstock.com

Discuss Juvenile Delinquency

The first step:

When first introducing the topic of juvenile delinquency, be sensitive and aware that very likely some—perhaps, many—of your students will be directly affected by it: either as victims or perpetrators of bullying, for example. A good way to broach such topics safely, while at the same time encouraging analysis of the literature, is to focus on the *character's* motivation. Don't ask, "Has anyone ever been bullied?" Or, even worse, "Has anyone ever been a bully?"

Instead, ask "Why do you think Tom Sawyer bullies the new kid? What is he after in this chapter?" Such questions get at the heart of the literary character's motivation and will inevitably lead the students themselves to begin to question their own behaviors and motivations. This is known as "bibliotherapy," but it's simply a natural process when encountering a work of literature to which the reader can relate.

The next step:

Supplement the fictional accounts of juvenile delinquency with actual, factual data. National statistics can seem vague or overwhelming; instead, keep it local: How many juveniles in your county have been arrested this year? Make it relatable: How many kids that are the same age as your students have been incarcerated? Be specific: What kinds of crimes are most common, and what are the sentences?

Guest speakers can provide a very personal perspective. If possible, you might invite a local law enforcement officer or counselor, a victim of juvenile crime, or even an adult who had been incarcerated as a juvenile.

The final step:

As a closing activity, raise questions for open discussion. Without making personal references to their own experiences, encourage your students to brainstorm solutions to the problem in general. Again, make connections to the literature: When Tom Sawyer encounters the new kid, what are some alternative behaviors? If Tom were your best friend, what would you say to him in this instance?

Lesson

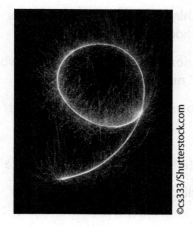

©cs333/Shutterstock.com

Research and Reflect

The first step:

A good teacher is always reflecting on the classroom experience, through both informal and formal assessment.

> What worked well?
>
> What surprised you?
>
> What would you do differently?
>
> What do you think your students learned?
>
> Did your students learn what you had intended; in other words, did you meet your objective?

Therefore, each of our four units will involve a short written reflection as a summative experience.

The next step:

After completing the fiction project, compose a thesis-driven 1,000-word essay incorporating outside research with your own reflection on the experience.

The bibliography listed at the end of this book contains a number of reliable outside sources, or you may prefer to consult the library or check additional online Web sites.

You may, if you wish, include quotations from one or more Newbery novels, but these are "primary texts" and do not count as "research" material.

The standard five-paragraph theme format is useful for such a short paper:

> ▶ State your thesis
>
> ▶ Support it with a brief quotation from one or two outside sources
>
> ▶ Briefly describe what you did in the fiction project....
>
> ▶ ... and what you learned
>
> ▶ Restate your thesis indicating that it is supported by your research and firsthand experience

Yes, it is permissible—even desirable—in a reflection essay to use the first person ("I").

Keep in mind that a thesis is not just a topic sentence: "This essay is about adolescent fiction." It contains both the topic and an opinion: "Fiction is an important genre of literature."

For this project, a possible thesis might be: "Adolescent novels can be used to introduce the topic of juvenile delinquency." It could be supported by quotations from your novel that represent juveniles in trouble.

The final step:

After drafting your essay, be sure that you have included proper citations for any quoted or paraphrased materials, following MLA citation format. The Purdue University Web site is a helpful resource for MLA format questions:

https://owl.english.purdue.edu/owl/resource/747/01/

Finally, proofread carefully for spelling, grammar, or punctuation errors.

Lesson

Prepare to Teach

The first step:

In the project that you completed for this unit, you worked with one novel and presented only a brief introduction to it. When you begin teaching, you will need to expand this project into a full weeklong unit plan—working your way through the entire book with a lesson for each day.

Your unit plan should open with a context statement or rationale for the unit. Before describing what you will do each day, step back and think about WHY you are presenting a unit like this. Why do you think it is valuable for your students to spend a week reading this particular book? And, in particular, why is it beneficial for them to be connecting it to the issue of juvenile delinquency?

Assume that you will devote one class hour to the lesson on each day. Then design the specific activities, along with your objectives or goals for what you hope your students will learn each day.

Be careful not to confuse "objective" with "activity."

> "Read chapter one."—This is an activity, something you will *do* with your students in this lesson.

> "Understand the five essential literary elements."—This is an objective, something you want your students to *learn* through the lesson.

The next step:

Design a daily lesson plan template that works for you. You can get ideas from Web sites or education manuals, but ultimately it is a matter of individual preference. Some essential categories to include are:

- ► objectives
- ► materials needed
- ► activities
- ► assessments

But whether you list them in this order or a different order, whether you put the information in boxes or columns, and whether the information is expressed in complete sentences or fragments in a bulleted list: all of this is up to your personal discretion.

A sample lesson plan is provided.

The final step:

Connect to core standards, as applicable in your state. You should consult the Department of Education Web site for current standards for your state. For example:

http://www.doe.in.gov/standards/englishlanguage-arts

Evaluation Sheet

NAME _____

This sheet MUST be submitted during your presentation!

	Poor	Satisfactory	Outstanding

OVERALL:

Choice of text

POWERPOINT:

Present the book clearly

Addresses all 5 literary elements

Appropriate graphics

NO misspelled words

GRADE: _____

𝓑𝒾𝒷𝓁𝒾𝑜𝑔𝓇𝒶𝓅𝒽𝓎

INTRODUCTION

Books

Bates, Laura. *Shakespeare Saved My Life: Ten Years in Solitary with the Bard.* Sourcebooks, 2013.

Campbell, Joseph, and Bill Moyers. *The Power of Myth.* Anchor, 1991.

Trounstine, Jean and Robert Waxler. *Finding a Voice: The Practice of Changing Lives through Literature,* U of Michigan Press, 2005.

Web sites

"Animal Cruelty and Human Violence." *The Humane Society of the United States,* [28 May 2016], *http://www.humanesociety.org/issue/abuse_neglect/qa/cruelty_violence_connection_faq.html*

"Tip Sheet for Teachers (Pre-K through 12): Incarcerated Parent." *Youth.gov,* [28 May 2016], *http://youth.gov/youth-topics/children-of-incarcerated-parents/federal-tools-resources/tip-sheet-teachers*

UNIT ONE

Books

Shakespeare, William. *King Lear.* Folger, 2005.

Spitz, Ellen Handler. *Inside Picture Books.* Yale, 2000.

Web sites

"Welcome to the Caldecott Medal Home Page!" *Association for Library Service to Children,* [3 March 2016], *http://www.ala.org/alsc/awardsgrants/bookmedia/caldecottmedal/caldecottmedal.*

"Common Mistakes to Avoid When Writing a Children's Book." *Quick and Dirty Tips: Helping You Do Things Better,* [3 March 2016], *http://www.quickanddirtytips.com/education/writing/common-mistakes-to-avoid-when-writing-a-childrens-book#sthash.2ZDDq2Cm.dpuf.*

UNIT TWO

Books

Bettelheim, Bruno. *The Uses of Enchantment*. Vintage, 2010.

Thompson, Stith. *Archetypes and Motifs in Folklore and Literature*, M.E. Sharpe, 2005.

Web sites

"Namibia." *Wikitravel: The Free Travel Guide*, [4 April 2016], *http://wikitravel.org/en/Namibia*.

"Multicultural Cinderella Stories." *American Library Association*, [4 April 2016], *http://www.ala. org/offices/resources/multicultural*.

"How the Zebra got its Stripes." *Gateway Africa*, [4 April 2016], *http://www.gateway-africa.com/ stories/How_the_Zebra_Got_his_Stripes_San.html*.

Save the Children. [4 April 2016], *http://www.savethechildren.org*.

"G is for Games." *Marie Pastiche: Exploring World Cultures With Kids*, [4 April 2016], *http://www.mariespastiche.com*.

TIME for Kids. [4 April 2016], *http://www.timeforkids.com*.

UNIT THREE

Books

Carroll, Lewis. *Alice's Adventures in Wonderland*. Bantan Classics, 1984.

Wood, David, and Janet Grant. *Theater for Children: A Guide to Writing, Adapting, Directing, and Acting*. Ivan Dee, 1999.

Web sites

"Alice's Adventures in Wonderland." *Carnegie Mellon University*, [5 May 2016], *https://www.cs.cmu. edu/~rgs/alice-table.html*.

"Alice's Adventures in Wonderland." *Project Gutenberg*, [5 May 2016], *http://www.gutenberg.org/ files/19033/19033-h/19033-h.htm*.

"Alice in Wonderland Extension Activities." *Scholastic*, [5 May 2016], *http://www.scholastic.com/ teachers/lesson-plan/alice-wonderland-extension-activities*.

UNIT FOUR

Books

Kaywell, Joan. *Adolescents At Risk: A Guide to Fiction and Nonfiction for Young Adults, Parents, and Professionals*. Greenwood, 1993.

Twain, Mark. *The Adventures of Tom Sawyer*. Dover, 1994.

Weir, Andy. *The Martian*. Broadway Books, 2014.

Web sites

"Adventures of Tom Sawyer." *NEA Big Read*, [15 May 2016, *http://neabigread.org/teachersguides/lesson_plans/adventuresoftomsawyer*.

"Newbery Medals and Honors." *American Library Association*, [15 May 2016], *http://www.ala.org/alsc/awardsgrants/bookmedia/newberymedal/newberyhonors/newberymedal*.

"Jacob Have I Loved." *Amazon*, [15 May 2016], *http://www.amazon.com/Jacob-Have-Loved-Katherine-Paterson/dp/0064403688/ref=sr_1_1?s=books&ie=UTF8&qid=1464456904&sr=1-1&keywords=jacob+have+i+loved*.

"Holes." *Amazon*, [15 May 2016], *http://www.amazon.com/Holes-Louis-Sachar/dp/0440414806/ref=sr_1_1?s=books&ie=UTF8&qid=1464456944&sr=1-1&keywords=holes*.

"From the Mixed-up Files of Mrs. Basil E. Frankweiler." *Amazon*, [15 May 2016], *http://www.amazon.com/Mixed-up-Files-Mrs-Basil-Frankweiler/dp/1416949755/ref=sr_1_1?s=books&ie=UTF8&qid=1464457081&sr=1-1&keywords=from+the+mixed+up+files+of+mrs+basil+e+frankweiler*.

"The Watsons Go to Birmingham—1963." *Amazon*, [15 May 2016], *http://www.amazon.com/Watsons-Birmingham--1963-Christopher-Paul-Curtis/dp/044022800X/ref=sr_1_1?s=books&ie=UTF8&qid=1464457052&sr=1-1&keywords=the+watsons+go+to+birmingham+1963*.

"The Martian." *IMDb*, [15 May 2016], *http://www.imdb.com/title/tt3659388/*.

Index